Amazing Journey:
Metamorphosis of a Hidden Child

by

Felicia Graber

To Phyllis
with my best
wishes
Felicia Graber
7/30/2023

Amazing Journey:
Metamorphosis of a Hidden Child

Parts originally appeared as the essay "And She Lived Happily Ever After" from *And Life is Changed Forever: Holocaust Childhoods Remembered*, edited by Robert Krell and Martin Ira Glassner. Copyright © 2006 Wayne State Univerisity Press, with permission by Wayne State University Press.

ISBN: 978-1-4515-4276-9
Library of Congress Control Number: 2010906861

Cover designed by Nehmen-Kodner: www.n-kcreative.com
Printed in the United States of America
by Felicia Graber
www.feliciagraber.com
feliciagraber@earthlink.net

Dedicated to ...

My husband, children, grandchildren, yet unborn descendants, and to the one-and-a-half-million Jewish children murdered during the Holocaust. May we always remember them and pass on our precious Jewish heritage.

Contents

" ... a man's suffering is similar to the behavior of gas. If a certain quantity of gas is pumped into an empty chamber, it will fill the chamber completely and evenly, no matter how big the chamber. Thus suffering completely fills the human soul and conscious mind, no matter whether the suffering is great or little. Therefore the 'size' of human suffering is absolutely relative."

Viktor Frankl
Man's Search for Meaning

"Feminism means the transformation of all society so that its organizing principle is not power and domination but rather the female values that are the core of Judaism."

Aviva Cantor
Jewish Women, Jewish Men:
The Legacy of Patriarchy in Jewish Life

Preface

"I survived" is a powerful statement, evoking many different emotions. When you think of or hear the word "survivor," all kinds of images spring to mind—positive ones and negative ones.

For me, the word "survivor" suggests that someone managed to stay alive during a man-made disaster—be it in Cambodia, in Africa, or in Nazi-occupied Europe. For Holocaust survivors, that word produces especially strong emotions. Who can legitimately call himself or herself a "survivor"? Some claim that in order to do so, you have to have been in at least one concentration camp, while others include anyone displaced or persecuted by the anti-Jewish decrees of the Nuremberg Laws.

The word "survivor" was one I struggled with for almost half a century. It never occurred to me to consider myself a survivor. After all, had I not been told over and over again that I was lucky to have been so young and that I could not possibly remember anything? But, as I grew older, I needed to seek out more details; I needed to go back to my hometown; I needed to find an explanation for certain fears and dreams I could not understand.

However, who needs another Holocaust memoir? A superficial search on amazon.com results in thousands of related titles. So, what makes my memoir different?

I am a "baby survivor" of the Holocaust, born after the Germans occupied my native Poland. I did not know I was Jewish until I was seven years old, nor did I know that the man I called "Uncle" was my biological father. I learned the story of our survival mainly from him.

He was a unique individual. He managed to guide my mother, me, and himself through the war years with minimal outside help. The three of us survived only because of his ingenuity and guts. He always managed to stand on his own two feet. No displaced-persons camps for us. He pulled himself up by his proverbial boot straps twice within the two years after liberation.

My mother was a heroine in her own right. She managed to blend into a foreign environment along with me—her then-two-year-old daughter—and later hide her husband in our one-room apartment.

After the war, we moved from Poland to Belgium to Germany, and I later moved to England to finish my education. I went to school in five different countries and was instructed in four different languages. I changed schools nine times and graduated from high school at seventeen.

I spent my teenage years in Germany, one of two Jewish girls in a German public, girls-only high school with a student body of one thousand. At home I was swamped with stories of Nazi atrocities; in school I was surrounded by children of those who could have participated in them.

At nineteen, I married an American army chaplain; at twenty-three, already a mother of two, I accompanied my husband back to the United States, home for him but a new culture with different traditions, mores, and *Weltanschauung*—world view—for me. I was not exactly welcomed with open arms into his large family. I was the foreigner, the "greenhorn." I did not belong. In fact, the feeling of not belonging stayed with me for most of my life, no matter where I lived.

But I made it. I survived. After fifty years of marriage, I look back on a life that has been gratifying and fulfilling.

Foreword

Felicia Graber has written a remarkable memoir that holds the reader's attention from first to last. She calls her account "Amazing Journey," and so it was. What marks it out from many other accounts is that Felicia was born after the German conquest of Poland.

In 1933, seven years before Felicia was born, her mother fulfilled a youthful dream to go to Palestine, where she enrolled in an agricultural school, intending to cast her lot with her fellow pioneers. Unfortunately, after only a year on a kibbutz, she received a telegram to say that her own mother (Felicia's grandmother) was gravely ill, and she returned to Poland. Still hoping to return to Palestine, in March 1939 she married. Hitler invaded Poland that September. Felicia was born in March 1940.

Felicia was fortunate, despite being confined in the Tarnow ghetto, despite life in hiding, despite labour camp, she was never separated from her mother; indeed, both her parents survived. Liberation came two months before her fifth birthday. She recalls vividly "the roaring of the planes, the loud laughter of the drunken men stumbling down the road, the women crying and laughing." The young Felicia was confused and bewildered, but she was free.

Felicia's memoir takes us through post-war Poland and the coming of Communism there, and a "vacation" to Belgium, with the hope of a new life. It is a long and difficult journey to the United States, described in poignant detail: Belgium, Germany, England, and then the United States. While still in Germany, Felicia learns that President Kennedy has been shot. Three weeks later, she is on her way to Paris and Le Havre, boarding ship on December 18 and arriving in New York Harbour six days later, during one of the severest snowstorms in the city's history.

Felicia describes her life in the United States with fascinating detail, including two return journeys to Poland, the first in 1994, and the second in 2005. Her accounts of both visits are absorbing. On her first visit to the cemetery in Tarnow she found someone to restore her grandmother's grave. On her second visit, it takes her more than half an hour to clear the weeds so that she can come close to the tombstone.

Once more our knowledge of the Holocaust and its aftermath is enhanced by the courage of a survivor to set down an honest and perceptive account.

Sir Martin Gilbert
London, England

Introduction

In the beginning, there was Poland: Tarnow, Iwonicz Zdroj, Milanowek, Warsaw, Lodz, Sopot. Then, there was Belgium: Brussels; then, Germany: Bad Homburg and Frankfurt; then, England: Bentley; then, Germany again; then, the United States: Fort Hamilton, Fort Bragg, Ellwood City, Pittsburgh. Now, there is St. Louis. At the beginning, it was 1939. Now, it is 2010. Seventy years have passed, three generations have been born, a world war took millions of lives; and the Holocaust changed the face of humanity.

In the beginning, they were Blonders and Lederbergers, businessmen, watchmakers, goldsmiths, secretaries, dentists. At the end, they became Bialeckis and Grabers. Now, they are MDs, DDSs, rabbis, PhDs, CPAs, therapists, and teachers.

The journey was dangerous, treacherous, and were it not

for incomprehensible miracles, it would have all ended in 1942. That is the reason I am writing this book. It is not "just another Holocaust memoir." In fact, it is not primarily a Holocaust memoir at all. Rather, it is a legacy that I want to leave for my children, grandchildren, and yet-unborn great-grandchildren. I hope this will help them remember the past, protect the present, and pass on the history of a world that has disappeared—the world of Polish Jewry—to the next generations.

I hope it will also give educators, psychologists, sociologists, and historians insights into the psyches and problems of children when they grow up in unusually stressful times. Furthermore, I hope it will show young women that, no matter what obstacles life puts in their way, they can overcome them, they can grow to find who they are and have the courage to stand up and make their mark on society.

By the time Europe was liberated in the spring of 1945, six million Jews had been murdered. The first to be deported and killed were the elderly, the sick, the infirm, and the children—one-and-a-half-million children.

In Poland, where I was born, there were three-and-a-half million Jews in 1939. An estimated one million of them were children. According to historians, half-a-million adults but only a few thousand children survived. The vast majority of those children survived in hiding. Some were physically hidden; others hid their identities, taking on new names, religions, and families.

Some Jewish babies were taken in by convents, monasteries, or Christians families. After liberation, some children were able to reconnect with a surviving family member; others were taken to Palestine/Israel by Jewish agencies. Many, however, remained with the Christian families, often unaware of their parentage. In the course of deathbed confessions or neighbors' gossip, in the last decade, an estimated 25,000 young Poles found out that they were not Catholics, but Jews. Now, by posting notices on the Web, in journals, and in newsletters, they try to find anyone, anywhere, who might have any knowledge of their biological parents. I am one of the extremely fortunate baby survivors; I was never separated from my mother, and both my parents survived.

For decades, however, the Holocaust was far removed from my consciousness. I was sure that those early years of my life had no effect on me. I could not have been more wrong. As I grew older, this past started to haunt me. I became drawn to those years; I wanted to see those places. I wanted to know more, and my first trip to Poland in 1994 was a catharsis that changed my life.

This book, *Amazing Journey: Metamorphosis of a Hidden Child,* started as a project to transcribe and translate my father's twelve hours of taped oral history, which were the result of an interview he gave to Kenneth Jacobson in 1981. Then, a young reporter in Europe, Mr. Jacobson became interested in the fate of survivors and was doing research for his book, *Embattled Selves.* I received copies of these tapes, but stored them away in a drawer for years, where they remained untouched. My few attempts to listen to them never moved past the first two. Before that trip to Poland in 1994, however, I decided that it was imperative to listen to all of them and take notes.

Upon my return to the United States, I knew that my father's oral history had to be transcribed and translated from German into English for my children and grandchildren. It was not until 1996, however, when my brother, Dr. Leon Bialecki, underwent two major surgeries, that I started that long, arduous process. I wanted to tell my father's story but also to add my mother's recollections of her years living on Aryan papers. I wanted to include my own personal recollections as well.

I was overwhelmed by the amount of material I had accumulated and was at a loss as to how to proceed. It was my teacher and friend, Bobbi Linkemer, who convinced me that my own story, that of a "hidden child" of the Holocaust, as well as my accomplishments later in life, were just as important and worthwhile as my parents' and should be preserved.

It is my hope that my story, often full of half-recalled impressions and images, will help readers understand the impact past events have on our lives, no matter how young we are when they occur. They often remain as hidden as I was as a child.

Prologue: 1940 to 1942
Tarnow, Poland

My only connection to those two years is my father's and mother's stories. How I wish I could be hypnotized and sent back in time so that I might be able to recall the first two years of my life. How I wish I could reach the images in the deep recesses of my mind —pictures of grandparents who, I have been told, adored me. How I wish I could remember these very special people now long gone.

I was the first and only grandchild for both sides of the family, adored, fussed over, and spoiled. According to my parents, my grandparents came by daily, as long as it was safe, in order to hold me, to play with me. My paternal grandfather Leib Israel Lederberger's greatest joy was to have the opportunity to take me for a walk, to have me all to himself. He did not expect any other grandchildren. One of his two sons, Ted, had died as a teen; his daughter, Rachel, could not conceive; and his other son, my father, had married relatively late in life. So, I was "it"—the eagerly expected and yearned-for descendant, the one to carry on the family traditions, if not the name. What I would give to see him and talk to him for just a few minutes.

According to all accounts, the man was a tower of goodness, patience, tolerance, and devotion to his God, his wife, his children, and his neighbors. His son, my father, as well as his daughter-in-law, my mother, could not sing his praises often or loudly enough. They talked of the way he conducted himself in business, how he cared for his family, his generosity to all in need, his gentleness, and how he was able to soothe the most heated argument.

I have only one photo of him, a picture salvaged by my great-uncle, Adolph, my grandmother Sarah's brother, who had fled burning Germany and settled in New York. This picture, probably taken in the early 1930s, shows my grandfather with his wife, Sarah, and their daughter, Rachel, my father's older sister. He stands erect, head high, the picture of a grand, old gentleman. He has a short, black, neatly trimmed beard. He is wearing a black hat, a black coat over a black suit, a white shirt and black tie; and he is holding a black umbrella. Yet, there is nothing sinister looking about him. Maybe I am just imagining it, but his face seems to radiate the gentleness of his soul.

I would give anything to be able to hug my grandfather and see his soft smile, to feel his hand on my head, to look up into his eyes and tell him all about his wonderful grandson, Leon, who would be born after the war and named in his memory. I would tell him about Leon's and my children and my eight grandchildren. (Leon has no grandchildren yet.) How proud he would be of them, not only of their accomplishments but also of the wonderful people they have become. He would be filled with joy at their business sense, their decent characters, and their commitments to the traditions he cherished.

However, he was not even granted a natural death or a grave where he could rest in peace, a place where we could visit and find some solace. He was brutally shot while being loaded like an animal onto a German army truck because his rheumatism did not allow him to move fast enough to please his captors. His crime? He was a Jew, an "old" man of sixty who was useless as a productive slave laborer to the Germans.

My grandmother, who is standing next to my grandfather in this picture, is a head shorter than he is. It is difficult to see her face because she is wearing a hat, which partially covers her features. She, too, wears black and white—a black dress with a white ascot-like scarf. I can almost see myself in her. I have the same build, the same demeanor. According to my father, she was a very strong woman, sometimes too hard on her family, but respected by all. She adored me, her only grandchild. She most likely met her death in the Buszyna Forest, about six miles from Tarnow, where thousands of elderly Jews and young children were shot and dumped in a mass grave on June 11, 1942.

The third person in that picture is Aunt Rachel. As I was

growing up, I was often told that I resembled her, although she is taller and has a much slimmer build. She was married to Jacob Kresch and lived in nearby Nowy Sancz. Her fate is unknown. She and her husband vanished along with the other six million martyrs.

I do not have a picture of my maternal grandfather, Simcha. My mother described him as a distant, strict man, very committed to his religion and its traditions. I know very little about his background or his life, as he did not seem to have communicated well with his children.

I do have a picture of my maternal grandmother, Fani (Feiga), who died in 1934. She was a beautiful, distinguished-looking woman, prematurely gray. Her eyes were large and sad; her demeanor, however, displayed a grace similar to that of my mother. She was adored by her three children, who put her on a pedestal and considered her a saintly woman.

Those are the people I would want to meet—people I heard about all my growing-up years; their traditions, thoughts, ideals, and values have been transmitted to me by my parents. I, in turn, have passed them along to my children and grandchildren in spite of the Nazis' attempts to annihilate the Jewish people.

I also want to paint a portrait of my parents as I remember them. Whenever I open my jewelry drawer, I see my mother's pearl earrings and recall them framing her small, delicate, finely chiseled face, highlighting her olive complexion, and adding to her refined air. Her black eyes and hair and her simple hairstyle completed her almost Hispanic appearance. Those beautiful eyes never seemed to smile, however; and the slightly drooping corners of her mouth added to the poignancy and sadness of her face. I seldom heard her laugh or saw her lips turn up in a genuine smile; but, when she did laugh, her eyes glowed with a brilliant light.

There was something elegant and noble in her bearing. During the last years of her life, her black hair was speckled with gray; yet, her almost wrinkle-free face belied her age. Lipstick and a light dusting of face powder were the only touches she used to enhance her features. She dressed simply, preferring classic, ageless styles to current fads. However, she always wore her jewelry—nothing showy but, rather, tastefully small and elegant pieces. And she always wore her small pearl earrings.

My mother did not have a happy life. Brought up in a strictly traditional Jewish household in Tarnow, Poland, she rebelled early against the obligatory Orthodox restrictions of her family. Her dream was to go to Palestine, to learn farming, and to join a *kibbutz*, a collective community. She had a brief taste of her dream in 1933, when she joined a group of young men and women and enrolled in an agricultural school in the land of her ancestors. I think that year was probably the happiest in her life. Even in her eighties, she would still talk about it, recalling the dirty, strenuous work with love and nostalgia. She would describe her friends, her teachers, the summer heat, and the dreams she had had for her future. She was going to spend the rest of her life rebuilding this ancient land, working side by side with other young pioneers.

But, then, in early 1934, the telegram came. Her mother, whom she adored, was gravely ill. Her days were numbered, so my mother packed a few necessary things and made the long trip back home to Tarnow. She fully intended to return to Palestine; she believed the pioneer existence was her destiny. Life, however, had other plans for her. Her mother died soon after her return in the fall of 1934. Her sister, Adele, and Adele's baby died a few months later during childbirth. My mother and her brother, Ignaz, felt the double blow intensely. How could she leave Ignaz all alone when he needed her support and help? So, she got a job as a secretary and remained in Poland. I believe, however, that she never fully gave up the hope of going back to the Land of Israel.

In March of 1939, she married my father, and her future seemed to look up. But again, fate intervened: a few months after her wedding, on September 1, Hitler invaded Poland. By the time I was born, the following March, life had become a struggle.

Every day, the German occupiers imposed new restrictions on the Jewish inhabitants. My parents were forced to leave their beautiful apartment, the new linens, and the barely two-year-old furniture. My mother and father could only take with them whatever they could carry. This was just the beginning of a long and dangerous journey that would propel them both into a perilous world where a wrong word or gesture could mean the end of life.

Whenever I look at my face in the mirror, I see my father's face—round, light-skinned, and covered with freckles the moment the sun touches it. My eyes have the same shape as his—rather small, oval, and set close together. In fact, it was my face staring back at me in the mirror one day in my early teens that convinced me that Shlomek, as my mother always called him, was indeed my biological father.

The older I get, however, the more I recognize that I have inherited more from him than just the shape of that face and body build. I realize that my stubborn streak, of which he used to accuse me, also came from him. He always went his own way, followed his own logic. Once he decided on a plan of action, he was set. He usually did not waver, nor was he easily persuaded to change his mind.

He trusted people to a fault, never believing that anyone would deceive him, trick him, or act other than honorably. That was his way. He had a very strong sense of justice, honesty, fairness, and love for his fellow humans. He would have tears in his eyes when he talked about something that had touched him or when he watched a sad movie.

He loved and admired beauty, be it the physical beauty of a woman, a gem, or a piece of jewelry. He was a goldsmith by profession, but beautiful jewelry was also his hobby and his passion. As soon as I was old enough, he loved to surprise me with gifts of jewelry, and it gave him great pleasure to see me wear them.

During the war years, he became a hero. He helped anyone he could, sometimes taking chances, which threatened his life, as well as my mother's and mine. Those war years, however, were in a way the noblest of his life. He neither could not nor would stop talking about them. No matter where a conversation started, it always ended with what he had done during the Holocaust.

As a child and a teenager, I dreaded those talks. I often wanted to leave the room and never hear his stories again. Nevertheless, there was no stopping him; the war years lived with him until his death in 1991.

My personal memories from the war years are confined to scenes that appear in my mind, often without rhyme or reason. I have always claimed that, unlike many of my peers, I was and still am a very lucky woman. Even my name, "Felicia," comes from the Latin word for "luck" or "happiness." In fact, the war years were for me a breeze compared to those of other Jewish children. I was never separated from my mother; both my parents survived and filled in the blanks of the first seven years of my life. Growing up, I was told over and over again how lucky I was to have been such a young child during those war years ... lucky, because I could not possibly have any memories of the terrible things that happened ... lucky, because I do not remember hunger or fear.

Sometimes, though, I wish I did remember. When I talk to older child survivors who remember their grandparents and happy scenes from their early childhoods, I wish I, too, could picture scenes of the "life before." I wish I could see my mother as a young woman and a wife. I wish I could recall my hometown of Tarnow as it was then, a small town where Jewish life was strong and vibrant. I wish I could remember my father as a young man whose only worries involved running his father's prosperous jewelry business.

What I have are only some fragments and glimpses. Why do I only remember these little tidbits from my early years? I do not know, but they are entrenched in my mind and have haunted me throughout my life: mobs ... noise ... shouts ... trains whistling ... engines hissing ... screams ... dusk ... fumes ... people jostling to get on a train... a woman stretching her hands out of the window from inside the train, saying "Give me the child" ... another answering, "No, I'll not let go of my child."... Yet another woman, standing on the tracks, only her upper body showing, arms raised, crying out, "Please, take my baby."

A garden ... trees ... a white rabbit in a cage ... bullets flying through the window ... bombs exploding ... a soldier standing outside the door of the house, a rifle in his hand. I am just tall enough to see his black riding boots.

For years, I dream of a little girl riding alone on a train, of soldiers marching in goose steps. I have panic attacks in crowds and in train and subway stations. I freeze at the sight of riding boots and uniforms. I get frightened when I feel too happy, thinking that I do not deserve all this joy and that something terrible will happen as a result. I worry that the lack of nutrition and vitamins in my early years, as well as some unknown consequence of the typhus I contracted after liberation, will come to haunt me in my senior years.

I once read that the mouse and the snake are natural enemies. When a mouse comes face to face with a snake, she is so terrified that she freezes up, unable to run to safety, and is swallowed by the snake. Somehow, this story, whether true or not, has stuck with me over the years. In the late 1990s, when I first became involved in Holocaust-related activities, I often felt like that little mouse, fearing that I was being engulfed and devoured by those historical events.

I doubt these fears will ever disappear, and I know that, unintentionally, I have passed many of my anxieties to my children who will probably in turn pass some of them on to their children.

Acknowledgements

This book would never have happened were it not for the many people who helped me in the process. First of all, my deepest gratitude goes to my teacher, my friend, my editor, and my mentor, Bobbi Linkemer. Bobbi convinced me that I did have a story worthy of being written. She persuaded me that my writing was good enough and gave me confidence in my writing skills. She led me, pushed me, prodded me, organized my material. and acted as my computer coach. She read and reread my manuscript, edited, and made suggestions. In short, she is responsible for this book ever coming to fruition.

I am also indebted to Eva Shaw, writer and writing teacher. Much of the material in Amazing Journey is the result of my "homework" for her courses, as well as of her encouragement and confidence in my writing ability.

My thanks go also to Dr. Robert Hutcheson, teacher of the Holocaust Memory Project in St. Louis, whose workshops add a different dimension to my writing experience. Thank you to Dr. Martin Glassner and Dr. Robert Krell, who accepted my contribution to their anthology *And Life is Changed Forever,* which is excerpted in these pages.

Ken Jacobson's twelve-hour taped interview of my father's oral history was an invaluable source of information for which I am eternally grateful. In addition, Ken not only took the time to read my manuscript and make valuable comments and suggestions, he also graciously spent an evening with me going over each detail. His insightful questioning and probing into some aspects of my writing inspired me to delve deeper into myself. Although I was not able to include everything in this book, I am planning future articles that will explore some of his comments.

I want to express my deep gratitude to Sir Martin Gilbert for his encouraging telephone call, his patience through my search for a publisher, his great confidence in the merit of my work, and for taking time from a very busy schedule to write the complimentary foreword for *Amazing Journey.*

Thanks, too, to Bill Tammeus, journalist and author of *They Were Just People,* for taking the time to read and offer helpful advice. Dan Reich, curator and director of education of the St. Louis Holocaust Museum and Learning Center, encouraged me to start speaking to groups. He and Jean Cavender, director of the museum, made me feel a valued member of that organization, for which I am most grateful.

I would be remiss if I would not express my gratitude to all my friends and the members of our Hidden Child/Child

Survivor Group of St. Louis as well as the St. Louis Descendants of the Holocaust for their support, cooperation, and love which enabled me to a great extent to finally come out of hiding.

Last, but certainly not least, I want to thank my children Sarah and Steven, their spouses, Jonathan and Joy, and my grandchildren for their support.

To my beloved husband, Howard, I thank you for understanding the long hours I spend in all my Holocaust-related activities. I could not have done this without your cooperation and quiet encouragement.

Chapter 1: 1940 to 1944
Tarnow, Iwonicz Zdroj, Milanowek, & Warsaw, Poland

March 1940. I am finally born, just a few months after Hitler's invasion of Poland. I heard numerous times that I was almost not born at all. My mother was to have an abortion, like many of her contemporaries who were pregnant at the time. In fact, I understand that she already had an appointment with her doctor to perform the procedure. A pregnant woman cannot walk for miles to escape the Germans. And, besides, who wants to bring a child, especially a Jewish child, into these uncertain times? A baby means an additional burden, another mouth to feed, another body to hide. In hiding, a baby creates additional dangers. It cannot be kept from crying or making noises, which puts everyone in jeopardy. Many Jewish mothers smothered their infants to prevent their cries from alerting the Germans to their presence.

However, my mother did not have that abortion, partly because my grandfather begged her not to do it and partly because the physician was afraid of an electrical failure if the Germans bombed the nearby train station, as this would endanger her life. As a result, my parents could not escape to Russia. My mother was five months pregnant with me when many of their friends, including my uncle, Ignaz, left for the East. She could not undertake the long dangerous trek through forests to an unknown and uncertain destination.

The first time I heard this story was during my initial attempt to listen to my father's oral history tapes in the late 1980s. I broke down sobbing; I had immense feelings of guilt and believed I was responsible for preventing my parents from fleeing Poland.

June 20, 1942. We have to move to the ghetto. We are taken in with my parents' friends, the Osterweil family of four. They have a room in the Michalewicz House, a former Jewish cultural center. It is here that my father finds and organizes two important hiding places for those who cannot always keep up with all the ever-changing German regulations. Those hiding places, which can be accessed only from our room, will play an important role in our lives.

September 10, 1942. It is the morning before the eve of Rosh Hashanah, the Jewish New Year, and I am two years old. The second deportation in the ghetto is under way. Again, this is an event my father tells and retells throughout my growing-up years. I can still hear his voice as he describes his anguish in the decision-making process, tears often running down his cheeks.

All Jews have been ordered to assemble on the city square early in the morning. Papers are checked. "Where do you work?" "Do you have the correct stamp of the week issued by the occupying forces?" We are safe. My father always manages to have the correct documents. However, something goes wrong; we are not being released and allowed to go back to our one-room apartment. The Germans are altering the rules again. Thousands of men, women, and children are kept on the square all day. Hungry and thirsty, the children are crying. Mothers and fathers try to calm them, to distract them. But they cannot calm their own fears. "What is going on? Why we are not allowed to go home? What now?"

The sun is setting. It is getting dark. Suddenly, a German officer yells through a megaphone "Silence!" As one, the crowd falls quiet and listens. "All children are to come forward," the German yells. "They will be taken to another town—a more pleasant and healthier environment. Mothers with small children may accompany them if they wish." "Schnell, schnell," he continues. "Let's move."

Chaos breaks out. People are asking each other, "What does that mean? Where are they taking our children? Should we go with them? Should we let them go alone? Are the Germans to be trusted? Are we to offer our children as a sacrifice and save ourselves? Or are we to go with them? If we go along, we are just giving them more victims. We need to save ourselves; we can rebuild a family later."

That is what my father is thinking; he always likes to follow his logic. He puts me on the truck, grabs my mother's hand, and drags her away. But I start crying. I do not understand why my parents are leaving me here with strangers. I scream. My parents stop dead in their tracks. They cannot do this. My mother frees herself from my father's grip, runs toward me, and climbs on the truck. My father follows. "You stupid fool," says the German guard. "If that is the way you want it, go ahead."

It takes years for me to come to terms with the fact that my parents almost gave me away to the Germans. I must confess I felt deeply angry, upset, resentful, and hurt that they even thought of sacrificing me. This is a part of my experience that, to this day, I never mention when I speak about the war years. The first time I put this incident on paper was during a writing workshop at the Detroit Child Survivor Conference in 2006.

I do remember, however, the day when I finally came to terms with that episode. I guess, it was one of those "aha" moments when, after having put this occurrence on paper, I came to realize that what really counts is that my parents could not bring themselves to give me up; that whatever they had meant to do, in the final analysis, they had not abandoned me. I finally was able to comprehend that it is impossible for anyone, including me, to stand in judgment of those who were put in such a situation where they had only seconds to make such dreadful decisions. My parents, after their initial attempt to save themselves, were willing to sacrifice their lives in order to reassure and console me. Because of their action, not only am I alive today, but so are thirteen other beautiful human beings—my two children and eight grandchildren and my brother Leon and his two sons.

The fact that my father joins my mother and me on that truck saves all our lives. He is pulled from that transport because someone intervenes on his behalf. He is able to take my mother and me back into the ghetto with him. The reason for our release is that one member of the *Judenrat*, the Jewish Council, has a mother and sister hidden off our room. If we were deported, the hiding place would eventually be discovered and its occupants shot. This man manages to convince the German ghetto commander that my father is an indispensable member of that puppet government. So, instead of being deported to Auschwitz the next morning, we are taken back to our room in the ghetto.

It is then, after this miraculous deliverance, that my father goes into action. He arranges for a forged I.D. for my mother and a baptism certificate for me. He bribes someone to smuggle us out of the ghetto and drive us to Iwonicz Zdroj, a resort town near Tarnow, to live as Aryans. How does he manage that? The only explanation he gives is, "I got it from my underground connections."

My mother, Tosia bas Simcha, born and raised in a strictly Orthodox Jewish family, somehow manages to survive among the Poles. Most of my life, I never truly appreciated the task my mother undertook at the time. She had led a relatively insulated Jewish existence, dreaming of a pioneer life in Palestine. She would have had very little contact with non-Jews; yet, she is now thrown into a Catholic world she knows nothing about. I have no idea how my mother man-

ages to blend into Polish society as she does. Growing up, I
never thought about asking her.

With her two-year-old child, she lives for three long years
on forged Aryan papers. She first finds a room in Iwonicz
Zdroj, then has to flee to Milanowek, not far from Warsaw
because I compromise our situation by telling one landlady
that "my daddy's name is Shlomo," a typical Jewish name,
and another that I am "Catholic, but really Jewish." At one
point, Mother is so desperate for a place to live that she considers giving herself up to the Gestapo and ending it all. But
she does not. Like a true *Aishes Chayil*—a woman of valor—
she keeps going.

It is hard to imagine how difficult it must have been for
her to learn, and then to train me, how to act like a good
Catholic or how to behave in church when we finally find
refuge in Warsaw. She teaches me the "Lord's Prayer," which
she recites with me every night, and takes me to mass every Sunday. She transforms me into a devout Catholic girl. I
cannot even fathom how she feels about her daughter em-
bracing Catholicism with such fervor—her Jewish daughter
for whom the highlight of the week is to go to mass and to
push her way to the front of the church so she won't miss
anything.

Except for a few rare meetings with a Jewish man who is
helping other Jews in hiding, my mother is left to her own
devices. She has to fend for herself. She has to learn how to
behave in a foreign environment and what to say to whom.
She has to watch her every word and every gesture lest an
eager Pole become suspicious and denounce us to the Gestapo. She has to invent a credible past to tell curious neigh-

bors, and she has to ingrain in me that "Daddy's name is Josef Slusarczyk. He is a Polish soldier who fought against the Germans and is now missing in action." She has to teach me what can or cannot be told to strangers or friends.

The one communication she has with Father is through a Polish farmer, Marian Urban, who travels every two weeks from Tarnow to Warsaw, about two hundred miles, to bring her news from her husband, as well as a piece of jewelry to sell on the black market so that she can pay for food and rent.

Fall 1943. Father escapes from the ghetto with the help of a German officer and joins us in Warsaw. He arrives dressed in a railroad-worker uniform, a disguise used as a safety measure, since a government railroad employee has less chance of being checked carefully. His new name, according to his documents, is Andrzej Bialecki, not Josef Slusarczyk, as I have been told. I do not recognize this man whom I have not seen in about eighteen months. He is introduced to me as a friend of my father, and I am told to call him "Uncle." He needs a place to live. He cannot rent his own room as it is too dangerous for him to make the mandatory visit to the Polish police station to register. He does not have my mother's "good Aryan" appearance, and his Polish is often speckled with a Yiddish twang.

So, it is up to my mother to hide him in our one-room apartment behind a large wardrobe and train me that "nobody lives with me but my mother." Decades later, my mother still recalls how she would wake me up in the middle of the night to ask "Who do you live with, Felusia?" And only when I would respond "I know. I live only with my mother ... no one else," would I be allowed to go back to sleep.

In spite of it all, she takes a tranquilizer every time I go out to play with the other children and interrogates me about who said what to whom upon my return. All my growing-up years, I am told that I was literally "pulled out of Hitler's clutches" and had my parents' lives as well as my own in my hands at the age of four.

Chapter 2: 1944
Warsaw & Pruszkow, Poland

August 1, 1944. The Polish Home Army starts a revolt against the German occupiers on August 1, 1944. The Poles want to liberate Warsaw themselves and avoid being subjugated by the Russians. The Red Army already stands at the east bank of the Vistula River but will make no attempt to support the Poles. It is an uneven fight, with a poorly armed guerrilla force pitted against the still mighty German *Wehrmacht* (army).

One summer night, the lights are turned off, and I can see the dark-blue sky as I peek from under our only bed where my mother and I are crouching. I hear the rumble of planes and see bullets flying into the room though the open window. The next day my mother and I are huddled in the basement with the other tenants of the building. There is a boy there. He is sickly, pale. He has a blanket draped around his shoulders. We play quietly. For me, all this is part of life. I do not know any other existence.

October 2, 1944. The revolt is crushed. The Polish fighters surrender. We must leave the house where we have been living for the past two years. I am holding on to Mother's hand. There are masses of people in the street, all walking in a long human caravan in one direction. At the door of the house my eyes stop on a pair of legs in high black boots. As I look up to the tall man, I see his riding pants and his green German uniform. He stands there, a rifle in his hands, watching us join all the other people as they are herded away from Warsaw by the German army.

I don't remember hearing any noise, though, years later, I find out that the Germans blow up the houses as people leave them. Mother, Uncle, and I are walking in this human column. We walk and walk and walk. I have no idea for how long. Finally, we arrive at a camp, our destination, near the town of Pruszkow, about thirty-five miles southeast of Warsaw, where the Germans had established *Dulag-Durchgangslager* (transit camp) #121.

When we enter the camp, we are separated into two groups, men on one side, women and children on the other, with German soldiers patrolling the space between. I, of course, am with Mother. She sends me over to the men's side with something to give to Uncle. One of the soldiers looks at me and waves me through. I run to the men's side and then back as fast as I can. Then, Mother gives me something else to take to him. Again, the soldier waves me through. When Mother tries to send me back a third time, however, the soldier barks, "If you do this again, you will stay with the men. You will not go back." I rush back to Mother, petrified. At night, I lie on a cement floor, my head resting on a small suitcase. I am cold, shivering. I cannot get warm. Years later, doctors trace the pains in my shoulder to those days.

For years, I have flashbacks of this scene, but cannot pinpoint where it took place. Then, one day, I read *The Lost Childhood, a World War II Memoir* by Yehuda Nir. Professor Nir's Holocaust experience is similar to mine; however, he is ten years my senior. He describes the fighting in Warsaw and the conditions in Pruszkow camp. "Each of the arriving refugees was given a small area of filthy, oil-soaked cement floor to spread his belongings," he writes. There. That is the cement floor!

We spend what seems like an eternity in this place. In reality, it is only a few days.

Chapter 3: 1944 to 1945
Chyliczki, Poland

Fall 1944. From Pruszkow, most able-bodied men and women are shipped off to Germany for slave labor; thousands of others are sent to Auschwitz. For some unknown reason, the Germans decide to free women with small children up to the age of two, and my mother convinces a German guard that I am two. I am very small and they believe her.

Uncle puts his arm in a sling, claims to be injured and to have dysentery. He is quarantined in a make-shift hospital tent. When the "sick" are being evacuated to what is supposedly a "hospital," he manages to sneak away. Mother and Uncle —though separated—have the same thought: "Let's get away from this area, away from this camp, as quickly as possible. Let's take the first available train no matter where it is headed." By accident or fate, the three of us—Mother, Uncle, and I —are reunited on a local train. Although their joy at this unexpected reunion is great, they keep their emotions in check to avoid alerting fellow passengers that anything unusual is going on.

When the train arrives at the end of the line, we find ourselves in the middle of farm country where small, scattered, wooden houses are connected by dirt roads and form tiny villages. The fierce Polish winter is around the corner, so our immediate need is to find shelter, perhaps with a farmer who is willing to let us sleep in his barn. Years later, I find out how vital it is that our true identities not be discovered, as many Polish peasants are anti-Semites. The Germans will also shoot an entire Polish family if anyone helps a Jew but reward its members with extra food rations if it turns in a Jew.

The first farm family that allows us to sleep on the straw in its barn does so reluctantly. At first, we get no sheets or blankets. When Uncle convinces the farmer's wife to loan us some linens, they are covered with lice. Mother promptly starts to launder the sheets, which brings out the wife's ire. "You are ruining my sheets by washing them," she yells. "I will not allow this. I am taking them all back." This situation is untenable, so the search goes on for friendlier hosts.

Accidentally, we come across a very generous family, the Sierocinkis. The couple and their two daughters, sixteen-year-old Wladka and eleven-year-old Janina, live in the tiny village of Chyliczki in a wooden, two-room house without indoor plumbing or electricity. They take us in, share their meager food supply and tight sleeping quarters for the next five or six months. They demand nothing in return except some help in the field and the house. I remember very little about the Sierocinki's farm. What I do remember is the cow. My job on the farm is to watch the family's only cow. It is their prized possession. One day, in late October or early November, the weather is still warm, and the sun is shining. The cow is grazing peacefully. I am told to watch her and make sure she does not wander into the cornfield. I am given a big stick to help me control this giant creature. I am four years old and barely three feet tall. The cow is huge. All goes well until the cow starts making her way slowly into the forbidden field. I panic. I do the only thing I can think of: I stand behind her and hit her on her rump with my stick. Of course, the more I hit her, the further into the field she goes. Finally, I realize that this is not working, that I am totally helpless. I run back to the farm in tears seeking help.

Chapter 4: 1945
Chyliczki & Lodz, Poland

January 18, 1945. Liberation. Planes are roaring overhead. People are dancing in front of their homes. Men are strutting drunkenly down the unpaved street, laughing, singing, and shouting, "The Russians are here! The Russians are here!" Uncle is one of these men and, as usual, the center of any celebration.

I am almost five. I am confused. I am not sure what it is all about—the roaring of the planes, the loud laughter of the drunken men stumbling down the road, the women crying and laughing. It is all bewildering.

That spring, Uncle takes off, looking for a location where we can restart our lives. He finds a room for us in a big city. It is called Lodz and is about ninety miles southwest of where we are. We live in an attic-like place with a long set of steps. It is here that I become very ill. First, I get typhus. The doctor insists that I be hospitalized, but Mother refuses. "I did not go through the whole war with my child to be separated from her now. God only knows what they will do to her in the hospital," she says. The only way it is feasible to keep me at home, according to the doctor, is for her to quarantine herself with me and have no contact with the outside world for six weeks until I recover. She agrees.

Later, I get ear infections, one after another. I remember those. There is so much pain. Uncle carries me for what seems like endless nights. One horrible day, the doctor looks in my ear, and I feel a sudden knife-like shooting pain throbbing through my whole body. He has pierced my eardrum to let out the pus.

Fifty years later, I go to the doctor because of an ear infection. He looks in my ear and tells me, "Your ear drum has been punctured." "How do you know?" I ask. "I can see the scar. It is still there," he says. So, the pain was real. I am not imagining these things. It is so difficult to separate dreams from reality.

Summer 1945. Uncle leaves us again, this time, to look for a town where he can find a shop and the tools he needs to open a watchmaker store. Somehow, he finds a way to let Mother know that he found what he needed in Sopot, a small town on the Baltic Sea. Anxious, mother decides not to wait any longer for him to come and get us. She packs our few belongings, and we go to the train station. It is mobbed.

People are yelling, calling to each other, trying to make themselves heard over the racket. They are pushing and shoving to get on a train and not be left behind. The whole world seems to be going somewhere. The engines are whistling. What commotion. I am petrified. (To this day, I am anxious in train stations, and frightened by the sound of the whistling engines.)

Mother and I arrive safely in Sopot, a beautiful resort town about two hundred miles from Lodz. We go to a large apartment and are taken into a spacious bedroom by an old lady. Facing me is a gigantic bed covered with a gold-colored spread. At the foot of the bed is a small single bed. But the most exciting sight is a doll. She is sitting in the middle of the big bed. She has long black curls cascading down her back. She wears a pink satin gown trimmed with black lace, and on her head is a wide-brimmed pink hat, which is also trimmed with black lace. I have never had a doll before, and she is beautiful, dressed like an antebellum southern belle.

I rush in and take her into my arms. I feel absolute joy but never play with her. My life to this point has not included playing with any toys. I do not know what you do with a doll. My reality has not included seeing mothers taking care of young children.

Chapter 5: 1945 to 1947
Sopot, Poland

Fall 1945. We are now in Sopot. Uncle has launched a business here, and life is becoming nicer. He has taken a photograph of me. In it, I am five years old. It is a chilly, cloudy, and dreary day. I am standing on a pier. The North Sea in the background adds to the dark mood of the shot. I can feel the cold wind blowing through my hair. I am holding my black-and-white checkered coat closed with my hands clasped in front of me. A big white bow sits on top of my hair; white knee-socks and ankle-high, lace-up shoes complete my outfit. The coat does not provide much warmth. The grimace on my face reflects the weather and my mood, but it is the best I can muster when my mother tells me to smile. I am not happy at all. But I should be happy. The war is over. We have a nice apartment. I have a doll, and we even have a dog.

Soon after we get settled in Sopot, Uncle acquires a magnificent dog. His name is Tommy. I am enthralled, although Tommy is not really a pet. He is a highly trained, ferocious-looking German shepherd. He is a guard dog and a protector. Poor Tommy has a hard time adjusting to his new surroundings. He mourns his old master, walks with his head hanging low and his tail between his legs. He refuses any food. He needs time to readjust. The trouble is that I am impatient. I am so excited to have a dog. I want to watch him eat.

So, the second or third day we have him, I grab Tommy's collar and try to pull him towards his food dish. He growls, turns his head towards my hand, and his fang catches the fourth finger of my left hand leaving a big open gash. Uncle hears me cry out, sees the blood, grabs a belt, and starts hitting Tommy until one of his paws is bleeding. Tommy crouches down, crawls under a table to avoid further beatings, and licks his wound. From this day on, however, he becomes fiercely attached to Uncle. He follows him like a shadow. He carries his briefcase to and from the store. When Uncle goes out of town on business, Tommy goes daily to the train station to wait for him. Then, if he does not find him, he comes back home and sleeps in the hallway where Uncle's coat is hanging.

For some reason, Tommy then becomes my special defender. He is ferociously protective of me. No one, not even Uncle, can come near me if Tommy feels I am threatened. Once, when Uncle makes believe that he will hit me, Tommy growls at him and menacingly shows his fierce fangs.

In the summer, Uncle wakes me up early every morning. He has bought a kayak and loves to take me out on the ocean. At first, we take Tommy with us to the shore, but he insists on swimming out to where we are. No matter how far we row, Tommy follows us. Uncle is worried that he will drown. Then, one day, Tommy catches up with us and tries to climb into the kayak, almost turning it over. That is the last time he is allowed to come with us to the beach. From then on, he must stay at home for everybody's safety.

As Polish prisoners are returning home, I keep urging my mother, "Come, let's go and see. Maybe Dad will come back." Finally, mother tells me that my father has been killed in the war and that she has married Uncle. According to her, I complain and tell anyone who is willing to listen, "I never saw a wedding. I was not invited." But I keep calling him Uncle.

June 17, 1946. My brother Leon is born. As my bed is still in the big bedroom, I hear Uncle accompanying Mother to the hospital. Leon is born ill. He has a hernia and rickets. A nurse is hired to take care of him. Mother is not well, either. She has been ill with Graves's disease for a long time but had refused surgery until after the baby's birth. Now, she is, first, preparing for the surgery, and, later, recuperating and regaining her strength.

I am in the care of Leon's nurse. She is an old, mean, skinny woman. I do not like her, and the feeling is mutual. She is supposed to take Leon and me for walks in the park so that he gets some needed sunshine; but, instead, she takes us to visit her friends where she parks the stroller in the court-yard of a building. I promptly report this to Mother, who has a serious talk with "Sister," as the woman is called.

The outcome of this talk? I am no longer allowed to go along on their walks. I am grounded. Mother has no choice. She cannot take care of the baby. She needs Sister. So, an au pair is hired to take care of me. She is a young woman. I am happy because she takes me to church on Sundays. Mother has stopped doing that, a fact I do not understand.

One day, when the au pair and I are walking, we pass a couple of men. They look different from the people we usually see on the street in Sopot. They have dark complexions, dark hair, and moustaches. "Those must be Jews," I hear my au pair say. This sounds dangerous to my ears. The word "Jew" seems to convey a sinister image for me.

December, 1946. For weeks, my au pair has been preparing me for a "surprise" for Uncle and Mother. I am to put on a Christmas show for them. On December 24, Christmas Eve, I am dressed in a white gown with a silver halo on my head and wings attached to my back. I am an angel, and I am to say a poem and sing a beautiful Christmas carol. I start, but in the middle, I stop. I cannot continue. My throat tightens. I cannot control my tears. Finally, I give up. Sobbing, I run to Mother. She hugs me and takes me on her lap. She turns to Uncle and says, "You would think the child knows."

Chapter 6: 1947 to 1950
Brussels, Belgium

The Polish Communist Regime is targeting all "capi-
talists." Life is getting too dangerous for us in Poland.
Uncle's prosperous store receives several surprise au-
dits from the financial authorities. Every few weeks, he is
assessed additional taxes and penalties. He tries to appeal,
to get help from highly positioned friends in Krakow but is
told that nothing can be done. The only way out is to leave
the country, if he can manage to acquire a passport and an
entry visa to a western state. He flies to Warsaw and bribes a
Belgian consul to issue us a visa to Belgium. Because Polish
authorities are still anti-Semitic, the passport has to be issued
under the name Bialecki, the name on his false identification
papers. As a result, we will never retrieve our original family

name of Lederberger. Uncle also exchanges all his available Polish zlotys for English pounds sterling, as these are more valuable, stable, and can be used everywhere in the western world.

June 1947. We pack our bags to go "on vacation" and catch a train for Brussels. While we wait for the train to depart, Uncle goes to buy a newspaper to pass the time. He is startled when he sees the headline, "The Consul of Belgium in Warsaw has committed suicide. He was caught taking bribes and was about to be arrested." Will we be stopped? Can the authorities connect us to this official? Luckily, nothing happens, the train takes off, and we are not stopped or questioned at the border as we leave Poland.

A new life starts for all of us, again. However, this new era begins on the wrong track. All the English pounds Uncle bought in Poland prove to be forgeries, printed by prisoners in one of the German concentration camps in an attempt by the Nazis to undermine the British economy. Unwittingly, Uncle bought them. Now, we are almost penniless, and Uncle has to start rebuilding our lives from scratch all over again. No more nurses, maids, or au pairs. No more beautiful, large apartment. We live in a dark two-room flat located half way underground. Our windows are at street level.

Fall 1947. We are in Brussels. I am seven years old, and I am anxious. I will be starting in a new school tomorrow— a school in a foreign country where teachers teach in French, not Polish. I will be in second grade, learning to speak, read, and write this new language.

We are sitting in the kitchen in our small apartment, which also serves as dining room, den, and living room. One bare bulb, hanging from the ceiling, is the only light. The four of us are sitting around an empty, square wooden table. Uncle and Mother sit facing me. My brother sits on Mother's lap. He is one year old and is wearing a blue knit bunting with a white top. Several times that day I heard my mother say, "You have to tell her. I do not want her to go to school without knowing." So, we are sitting here because Uncle needs to tell me something important, something that will change my life forever. I will never again go to church. I will never again smell the incense. I will never again push myself to the altar to be as close as I can to the priest.

I am told that I am Jewish, not Catholic. "We are Jews," says Uncle, "We had to pretend to be Catholic to protect our lives. I am Jewish. Your mother is Jewish. Your grand-mothers and grandfathers were Jews. Our whole family has been Jewish forever. And one more thing," he adds "I am not your stepfather or your uncle. I did not marry your mother after the war. You never had a father who was a Polish soldier killed while fighting the Germans. I am your real father. You are my daughter, just as your brother is my son."

As if in a trance, I go to the room where I sleep, take out the beautiful white and gold Catholic hymnal my au pair gave me as a good-bye present, and I tear it to pieces. There are no feelings attached to this action, no guilt or sadness. I do not, however, destroy my little gold pendant depicting Mary with her infant. That I keep for years to come in spite of being urged to get rid of it.

I have a harder time accepting the fact that "Uncle" is my biological father than that I am Jewish. I doubt that he is really my father. I keep thinking I am adopted. Then one day, about five years later, while combing my hair, I look up into the mirror, realize how much I look like him, and finally believe that I am his biological daughter.

In 1947, my parents have other worries, more pressing than the feelings of a seven-year-old child. They have to rebuild their lives for the second time in two years. Mother, still recuperating from her thyroid gland surgery, needs to take care of a sick baby. She is thrown into a new world again, one whose language she neither speaks nor understands. She is left alone for weeks at a time to fend for herself. Father has to find a way to make a living. Belgian authorities are quite willing to give political asylum to refugees from the Communist world but will not give them work permits. Belgium is rebuilding after the war and is not about to let foreigners take jobs away from their returning soldiers. So, Father ends up "commuting" to Germany. He spends months at a time there building a business, pulling himself up to make life more financially comfortable for us.

I have mostly fond memories of those years in Belgium. We move several times, each time to a bigger and better apartment. Each move also means a change of school. There is even a very brief stint in an Orthodox Jewish establishment—my parents' feeble attempt to teach me something about my newly found faith. It is an environment in which I am like a fish out of water. It is more than I can handle. My parents also cannot cope with the idea of having to comply with some of the school's religious requirements. And having to learn Hebrew in addition to French proves to be too much. So, I go back in the public school

During those four years in Brussels, I am put in charge of my brother and have to take him to the park every day after school. Even though I do not always enjoy being his nanny, I never rebel, never complain. Mother will tell me often in later years that I "never gave her any trouble." I am and always was a "good little girl," doing what I was supposed to do. If I resent having to walk and rock my brother to sleep for hours, I do not reveal it. I am well trained to do as I am told. I never let Mother know how frightened I am when she occasionally goes out at night and leaves me alone in charge of Leon. I lie in bed in the dark seeing all kinds of shapes that resemble people or animals. I am terrified; but I do not even consider putting on the light. Nor do I ever mention my fears to Mother.

Two boys my age—Ignaz and Bernard—are my only friends. Sons of Polish Holocaust survivors, they are refugees like us, the only people with whom my parents associate. We have no social contacts with any local Belgians, Jews or non-Jews. Every weekend we get together with the Wulkan and Weiss families. The adults take walks; the three kids talk and play. As Ignaz has a little sister who is my brother's age, the running joke is that our two sets of parents will exchange daughters, I will marry Ignaz, and Leon, my brother, will marry his sister.

However, these other families are in transit to other destinations—Argentina and Brazil—and too soon, they leave. Besides them, there is a neighbor's son with whom I play marbles. I have little contact with any girls from school, although once, when a group of us is walking home, one girl mentions her grandparents. I am startled. "Grandparents?" I do not know anyone who has grandparents. Grandparents are mythical beings, not real, living people in my world.

My favorite pastime is going to the movies. I am an avid movie fan, especially American movies. I am allowed to go to the movies every Sunday afternoon. I always go alone. That seems quite normal to me. It is also the highlight of my week. Some of my heroes are Burt Lancaster, Errol Flynn, Maureen O'Hara, and Yvonne De Carlo ... and, of course, Lana Turner in *The Three Musketeers*. I am so enthralled with that movie that I sit through two showings and come home two hours late.

I find Mother frantic. She is pacing in front of the house, waiting for me. She feels helpless and does not know what to do. She has visions of me disappearing and of never being able to find me. I receive a big lecture about responsibility and the fact that I must never do anything to give Mother problems. After all, I "was torn away from Hitler's henchmen," and I am "precious."

Once a week I get another treat. There is a bakery near us, and every Saturday I am allowed to pick a small pastry that does not cost too much. I have my eyes set on a larger one every week, but I never ask if I could possibly buy that coveted treat, just once.

Chapter 7: 1950 to 1956
Brussels, Belgium; Bad Homburg, Frankfurt, & Mainz, Germany

Father keeps trying to convince Mother that she must move the family to Germany. Commuting between Brussels and Frankfurt is just too much for everyone. Although Mother is not happy that our family is split, she is insistent: "I will not raise my children in Germany."

That year, Father reconnects with a first cousin, Tadek Brand, who survived the war. He is married now and lives in Munich where he is waiting for his papers for the United States. Uncle Adolph Rosenzweig, my grandmother's brother, who was able to leave Cologne in 1938, is sponsoring him. Mother is persuaded to travel to Munich to see Tadek and his wife, Sylvia, who just gave birth to a baby boy named

Mark. Father is asked to be the *sandek* (the godfather) to this newest member of the family, symbolizing renewal for the Jewish people. We find Munich a city in rubble. Very few buildings have not been touched by Allied bombs. Mother shudders and vows, "I will never move here. This is no place to raise my children."

However, one year later, in 1951, she capitulates; and we move to Germany. For the first few months we live in a small hotel in Bad Homburg, a resort near Frankfurt. Apartments are hard to find since most German cities have been heavily bombed. I like living here in this little town. The hotel is near a forest where I go to pick blueberries and strawberries. I also discover a new hobby—catching frogs. I find a large jar, which becomes their new home and which I keep in my room. That new interest comes to an abrupt end, however, when one evening I realize that my biggest bullfrog is missing. I turn my room upside down looking for him—in vain. That night I can hardly sleep, as I expect him to jump on me at any moment. The next morning I take my jar to the forest and let all the other frogs go free.

It is also here in Bad Homburg that I first meet an American. She is a young Jewish woman, married to a black American soldier. She has a most adorable little boy. She always appears sad and lonely. She and her baby are rejected by both her and her husband's families, as well as by the black, white, and Jewish communities.

Finally, Father finds a beautiful apartment for us in Frankfurt, and I even get to have my own room. The new dilemma is where to enroll me in school. A German school is not acceptable for Mother. How can she put a Jewish child in a German school? Who knows who the teachers are or what they did during the war? Besides, I would have to learn a new language, again. There is a French boarding school in Mainz, a town one hour away by train. It is a school for the children of the French occupying forces. Another Jewish girl—Renée, also a child survivor and two years my senior—attends that school.

So, I am enrolled in the Lycée Paul Tirard, and I room with Renée. Every Friday we take the train home to Frankfurt, and every Monday, early in the morning, we take the train back to school. Renée's uncle, who lives in Frankfurt, found her on a Polish farm after the war and adopted her, as neither of her parents survived. She and I never talk about the war years, never mention our pasts. We room together, are inseparable, but never broach that subject.

A few months later, another Jewish girl, Marielle, joins us. She survived the war in Budapest with her mother. We become "the inseparable three Musketeers." We room together, eat together, and study together. Although we do mingle with the other students during school hours, there is a special bond among us that we just take for granted. It is only about fifty years later, in 2000, when Renée and I attend the Conference of the World Federation of Jewish Child Survivors of the Holocaust in Seattle, Washington, that we finally talk about our pasts. We are amazed that we had never done so as teenagers.

In 1951, however, I am very unhappy at school. I am homesick; I cannot adjust. So, Mother gives in and enrolls me in Anna Schmidt Schule, a German private school. Her thinking is that a private school is a safer place. The school would be more careful about whom they hire as teachers. Well, on my very first day in school a tall man comes into the classroom. He has a crew cut, looks terribly stern, and is wearing riding pants and riding boots. When I see those, I freeze. He sounds menacing as he starts barking questions at me in German, which I have just started to learn. Sometime later that year, Mother discovers that ex-Nazis cannot get hired in the German Public School System, so many of them find jobs in private institutions. I am pulled out of Anna Schmidt and thrown back into the Lycée the following school year. Again, I last only a few months. Boarding school is not the answer for me. So, Mother reluctantly enrolls me in a public German girls' school —Elisabethenschule—where I actually manage to stay for the next four years.

Living in Germany means that I am in a constant emotional tug of war. At home, I continuously hear about German atrocities during the war; and, at school, my classmates are the children of those who might have committed them. I feel that I live in enemy territory. I cannot keep from thinking, what did my fellow students' fathers do during the war? I am psychologically cut off from my peers. I am incapable of making friends with my German classmates. There is an invisible brick wall between us. The school has about one thousand students, but I am one of only two Jewish girls. The other girl is much older and much more sophisticated. I have nothing in common with her, but she is the only one with whom I feel comfortable.

I spend weekends with my American movie magazines, cutting out pictures of my favorite stars, which I glue into a large notebook. I write letters to Hollywood and am thrilled when I occasionally receive an autographed photo. Every Sunday there is always the threat that I might be forced to go for a ride or walk with my parents and their friends. I hate those boring outings. Even staying home alone is preferable.

The situation at home is difficult. My parents, who never really had an opportunity to build a foundation in the early years of their marriage, are not able to do so now, either. Father and Mother cannot get together to establish a solid home environment. There is constant friction between them, and I become my mother's counselor, friend, and confidante. I am supposed to keep her company when my father is off playing cards with his friends. "You are a big girl, a smart girl. You should know better than to leave your mother alone at home. You know how lonely I am. Furthermore, how come you do not stand up for me to your father? After all, you are already a big girl."

That is a refrain I hear over and over again. I am also constantly reminded that I was "saved from Hitler's furnace," but I am never sure what I am obligated to do or what I owe to whom for my life. Mother does instill in me, however, that I must get an education, be able to "stand on my own two feet," and not have to rely on a husband to take care of me. She will to do anything, including sacrifice her needs, to help me achieve these goals.

On several occasions, I become the unwanted center of attention when my parents' survivor friends come to visit. One day, a man my parents knew in Poland comes to visit. Throughout his visit he keeps gawking at me. It makes me very uncomfortable. I cannot imagine why he is doing this.

When he leaves, I ask, "Why was this man staring at me like this? Did I do something wrong?"

"No," answers Father. "You did nothing wrong, but he had a little girl about your age who was murdered during the war. So, he cannot stop himself from looking at you and wondering what his daughter would look like now." I feel creepy. What did I do to deserve to live? Why was I alive, while this man's little girl was not? What did I have to do (or not do) to deserve this privilege? What I do not know is that this is a feeling shared by many survivors and is especially strong among child survivors. It is called "survivor's guilt."

In Frankfurt, in the early 1950s there is one significant event that affects my life. The Israeli government sends an envoy, a *shaliach*, to help the Jewish community and to instill a sense of Jewish and Zionistic identity in the generation born after liberation. That man, Jacob Oppenheimer, and his wife, Carmella, become my heroes and my friends. He introduces me to Israeli culture, songs, dances, and language, as well as to Freud and psychology. I am fascinated with that subject, which becomes my new hobby. We have weekly youth group meetings, and, although I am the oldest among the five or six Jewish children, it is my lifeline.

Jacob and Carmella show me that marriage can be a beautiful and meaningful relationship. They are also an Orthodox couple, so I get to see Orthodoxy in action for the first time in my life. Although I keep hearing stories about Jewish practices from my parents, we do not follow them at home. Our religious observances are confined to my mother lighting candles every Friday evening because, she says, "I made that promise to my mother on her deathbed," and going to the synagogue on *Rosh Hashanah* and *Yom Kippur*.

Another highlight of those years is my first trip to Israel. Mother finds out that her brother, Ignaz, survived the war, lives in Tel Aviv, is married, and has a little girl. In 1951, Mother decides to take me to visit him. We have a wonderful time in Israel. I learn a little Hebrew, just enough to somehow communicate with my little, newly-found cousin.

Throughout these years, however, unknown fears haunt me, intruding into my life unexpectedly. One beautiful spring evening in 1956, when I am sixteen years old, I am walking in downtown Frankfurt. It is rush hour. The streets are mobbed. People are rushing everywhere: some, to catch the streetcar home; others to make a last-minute shopping trip; still others, to take care of an errand they did not get to during the day.

The church bells of the Paulskirche start their customary evening ringing. They bellow over the whole area. Traffic is bumper to bumper. Impatient drivers honk their horns. It is getting dark. The sun is setting, but I do not see its beauty. I see only the darkness enveloping the city and the ominously dark clouds in the sky. I hear only the terrifying noises, which are all around me. My heart starts thumping. I could swear it is in my throat; it chokes me. I have trouble breathing. I want to get out of this crowd. I want to find a safe, quiet corner. I need to get to the security of home, the safety of my parents' presence. I elbow my way through the crowd to get to the streetcar stop, the streetcar that will carry me away from this tumult. Finally, one arrives. I struggle to get in. I will not be left behind. I will not wait for the next car. I just have to get home.

What is happening to me? Is it a flashback to that fateful evening of September 1942 when I was almost abandoned? Is it the fear of crowds, stemming from our trip from Lodz to Sopot?

Chapter 8: 1956 to 1957
Bentley, England

It is 1956. I am sixteen years old, and Mother decides that she cannot keep me in Germany any longer. So, she settles me in Pax Hill, an English boarding school. It is not a Jewish school as she had hoped, but rather a small international girls' school in Bentley near Farnham, one hour from London. We had first visited a Jewish school where mother planned to enroll me, but the facilities were horrible. In Pax Hill, I think I am the only Jewish girl, but what is most important for Mother and me is that it is not a German environment.

The school is the former estate of Lord Baden Powell, the founder of the Boy Scout movement. It is here that he held his first scout meetings. Pax Hill is a large, beautiful Eng-

lish Tudor mansion remodeled to accommodate a dozen or
more girls. There are dormitory rooms that house two girls
each, classrooms, a dining room, kitchen, and quarters for
Mr. and Mrs. Adams and their young daughter, Allyson. Mr.
and Mrs. Adams are the owners, directors, and principals of
the school.

My year at Pax Hill is great. I love it. It feels like liberation all over again. For the first time in as long as I can
remember I do not feel different. All the girls are different.
They are daughters of ambassadors, diplomats, and high officials from all over the world: Greece, Turkey, Saudi Arabia,
Malaysia, Thailand, India, Singapore, and Kenya, to name
a few. The girls, ages sixteen through eighteen, are here to
finish high school, to prepare for the entrance exam to Oxford or Cambridge Universities; to get a Western education,
which will attract a better match; or just to give their parents
some respite.

The plan is for me stay in Pax Hill for two years, the
first year to learn English and the second to prepare for the
General Certificate of Education (G.C.E.), the equivalent of
a high school diploma. Even though I have taken English as
a foreign language in Germany, my skills are poor. The plan
is for me to pass the language proficiency exam at the end of
the first year. The following year, I am to take the required
classes to prepare for the G.C.E. About two or three months
after school starts, however, I realize that I am wasting my
time. My English class is a joke.

I ask Mrs. Adams to place me in the courses with native
English speakers to prepare for the G.C.E. I would need to
pass a minimum of three subjects at the Ordinary Level and

two subjects at the Advanced Level in order to be eligible for
university. The curriculum is provided by Oxford University,
which also administers the tests each summer. Mrs. Adams
is very skeptical. "I do not think that this is possible, Felicia,"
she says. "That is just too difficult. You are setting yourself up
for failure. Your English skills are just not good enough."
But I am determined and insist. Mrs. Adams reluctantly
gives in, under one condition. "You still have to attend the
English for foreigners' class and take that exam. I do not
want you to finish the year here without any diploma what-
soever. As I doubt that you will pass the five requirements,
you will at least have something to show for the year." She is
adamant.

I suppose that she is also concerned about showing my
parents some tangible results. Tuition at Pax Hill is high. I
agree to her condition and enroll in Latin, English, and math
at the Ordinary Level and French and history at the Advanced Level. In addition, I continue to attend the English
for foreigners' class. I work very hard but enjoy my classes
and the friendships I develop.

There is Rosy from India, with whom I share the history class; Vita from Athens, who is there just to learn English and plans her future as a Greek society lady; tall, skinny
Marmieke from Holland, whose goal is to find the perfect
man in her life; and Leila from Saudi Arabia, a highly intelligent young woman whose parents forbid her any social
contact or outings off school grounds. I feel sorry for her. She
yearns for a Western life style, yet is destined to become a
traditional Muslim wife. Then, there is Daisy from Malaysia,
who works harder than anybody, determined to be admit-

ted to either Oxford or Cambridge University and become a physician. We develop wonderful friendships, which will last for several years. Vita even comes with me to Frankfurt during Christmas break, as her parents are too busy traveling, and she has nowhere to go.

I also meet a very nice elderly couple, Mr. and Mrs. Brink. They are friends of my mother's cousin. The Brinks are German refugees who somehow managed to get to England. I do not know how because we never talk about our backgrounds or our personal histories. They live in nearby Farnham, and I go to visit them from time to time for a friendly typical English afternoon tea. I will stay in touch with them for years, until they pass away in the 1960s.

Some highlights of that year include my few trips to London. I love that city, its history, literature, and shops. I go to the Old Vic Theatre where I am lucky to see Sir Lawrence Olivier in the *Merchant of Venice*. I am taken with that play, and shocked when I find out years later it is supposed to be anti-Semitic. To this day, I disagree with that assessment due to Shylock's emotional monologue in which he says:

"*. . . I am a Jew. Hath not a Jew eyes? Hath not a Jew hands, organs, dimensions, senses, affections, passions; fed with the same food, hurt with the same weapons, subject to the same diseases, heal'd by the same means, warm'd and cool'd by the same winter and summer, as a Christian is? If you prick us, do we not bleed? If you tickle us, do we not laugh? If you poison us, shall we not die?*"

Spring 1957. My parents' visa to the United States finally comes through. We all take the ship SS United States during my spring break and enter the States as legal immigrants. I meet my great-uncle Adolph, as well as my cousins and great-aunt Lina. I am disappointed in the city of New York. I had imagined that everything in America would be beautiful, modern, and clean. Instead, I find a hot, dirty, and often dilapidated city. Despite this, I do love it here in the States. I find the people friendly and warm. Everybody seems willing to help a stranger. Someone even goes to the trouble of walking with me to show me the way when I get lost in Manhattan.

The one thing I find interesting is how unaffected I am that we find family. I guess the term and meaning of an "extended family" is so foreign to me at the time that it does not even occur to me how wonderful it is to have found one. For me, family consists of my mother, father, and brother.

Within a couple of weeks, my parents take care of all the necessary paperwork that will allow us to reenter the United States within a year. We return to Europe—my parents and brother to Frankfurt and I to England to finish school. The plan is for Father to liquidate his business and for us to emigrate for good the following year.

As a special bonus I get to meet and speak with Ravi Shankar on the return voyage from the United States. He is a famous Indian musician. Only, I do not know that until I show Rosy my picture taken with him, and she starts screaming, "Do you realize who that is? He is the idol of all Indian girls." Oh well ... and I did not even get his autograph. To me, he was just a nice young man I met on the ship.

Chapter 9: 1957 to 1959
Frankfurt, Germany

Summer 1957. Contrary to Mrs. Adams' predictions, I pass all my exams, receive my high school diploma from Oxford University, and am eligible to go to college. My door to the United States is open, or so I think.

When I come back from England in the summer, I am told that Father's intention to liquidate his business is taking longer than expected. I am encouraged to be patient and to enroll in the University of Frankfurt while I wait for the family's move to the States. Well, I do as I am told, as usual. I become a student of international law in the local Wolfgang Johann von Goethe University.

There is no equivalent in Europe to an American college. When you finish high school, you need to choose your future career and concentrate on that field. Why do I choose law? I have always had very strong feelings about justice, a trait I might have inherited from my father. And, since I have no intention of staying in Germany, it seems only logical to pick international law. I naively think that justice and law go hand in hand.

Socially, that first academic year is not much different from my experience in the German high school, except that now I am able to mingle with foreign students. I join the Foreign Student Organization, where I am still the only Jew. I date a young Greek man for a short while, then, another from Holland. However, I have very little in common with these foreign students, and I never really feel comfortable among them. Dating a German is out of the question, of course. Again, I am a fish out of water; I do not fit in socially or academically. I am one of only a few young women in my class of hundreds. I have no idea what I am doing, and there are no counselors to help. I stick it out for about a year, totally lost.

I still have my Jewish youth group though, which has grown a little because some German Jews have returned to their fatherland—some lured by the financial incentives of the German government, others by sheer homesickness in spite of everything. In the summer of 1958, a Jewish summer camp is started for the children of survivors. Most of these children are born in displaced-persons camps shortly after the war. People are rebuilding families there. Men and women who have lost everything and everybody cling to each other, marry, and have children, demonstrating the unbelievable strength of the human spirit. As a result, there is a Jewish baby boom on German soil in the years after liberation. I become one of the counselors at that camp. At the time, I do not realize the miracle of life these youngsters represent.

Summer 1958. My parents let their visa to the United States lapse. Once again, I am stuck in Germany. I am determined, however, to bide my time and to work toward admission to an American college. I work part-time for a German-American professor who helps me with the necessary paperwork to apply to Barnard College in New York. I contact Ted and Sylvia Brand, my father's cousin and his wife, with whom we had reconnected in New York. They offer me temporary room and board, as well as any help in whatever I may need.

At home, things are not getting any better. My parents' relationship is strained, and I play a major role as Mother's support system and companion. Father and I have never become close.

Fall 1958. My arrangements to go to the States are taking shape. Even though Barnard College rejects me, I am sure I will be able to work something out. I even make a ship reservation. My parents, especially Mother, are not too happy about my plans. They are worried about sending an eighteen-year-old girl, alone, to the "new world." So, they come up with a scheme they know very well will work. They propose that, if I postpone my plans to go to the United States for one year, I can realize my dream of traveling. I can go to

Paris, Rome, Greece, and Israel, where I will be able to spend
the whole summer of 1959. Of course, it does not take any
effort on their part to convince me. I am willing to do anything for such an opportunity.

As the 1958-1959 academic year approaches, a few Israeli students appear at the university. They are sons of expatri-
ate Germans who have returned to their parents' homeland
to get a free education. We get together to form the first
Jewish student club in post-war Frankfurt, the "Israela." In
the meantime, I give up on law and am now a psychology
major.

Spring 1959. I receive the first installment of my grand European tour and spend two weeks in Paris, one of the cities of
my dreams. I love French history, French plays, and French
poetry. I find my way around Paris without help. I go to the
opera, to the ballet, to Versailles. I have the time of my life.
I have only one obligation. Every afternoon I have to report
to the Café de la Paix where a good friend of my parents,
Mrs. Schillinger, enjoys the traditional afternoon coffee. I
am supposed to tell her what I am doing, as well as my plans
for that evening and the following day. She is, in a sense, my
chaperone. I am more than willing to cooperate. I cannot
wait for the summer, for Italy, Greece, where I will see Vita,
and, of course, for Israel.

The day after I return from Paris, I receive a phone call
from a friend who works in the Frankfurt Jewish Community office. "I need a big favor, Felicia," she tells me. "There is
a young, American, Jewish soldier in my office. He can speak

only a few words of German and is determined to meet a Jewish girl who can show him around town. You are the only one I know who speaks English well. Can you help?" I consult with Mother, who suggests that we invite the young man for dinner to "check him out."

During dinner, the young American informs me that he has arranged for a double date with the two of us and the newly arrived American Jewish chaplain, First Lieutenant Howard Graber. He is also a bachelor and has just assumed his position to serve the American Jewish army personnel in the Northern Area Command headquartered in Frankfurt.

I have heard about that young rabbi from an American business friend of Father's. He had asked me to help the chaplain arrange some social function for the Jewish GIs and the few Jewish girls now living in Frankfurt. Of course, I say yes. I know that some girls go to services on Friday evenings for social reasons, to meet boys. I am not willing to do that. I am a romantic and an idealist; going to religious services in order to meet a boy seems irreverent and wrong. But, I am always willing to help in a worthy cause.

So, that evening of April 6 (yes, I do remember the exact date), I agree to go on that double date. When I meet this young rabbi, it is love at first sight. I have been brought up with stories of European rabbis. I understand that they are to be honored, revered, followed ... but dated? That does not even cross my mind. So, when Howard Graber calls me for a date a few days later, I am in shock.

Eight months later to the day, we are married.

Chapter 10: 1959 to 1963
Frankfurt, Germany

In spite of the lack of a traditional Jewish lifestyle in my upbringing, I have absolutely no problems slipping into Howard's Orthodox customs. He never asks me to observe his practices; I just naturally adopt many of them. My parents are surprised. When Father asks me to do an errand for him on a Saturday, I politely refuse, saying, "Dad, I have decided to observe *Shabbat*." He looks at me and smiles, "Just because you are dating a rabbi does not make you a *rebbetzin* (a rabbi's wife)," he observes. But he never again asks me to do anything that would violate that holy day.

June 1959. Howard's cousin Ceil comes to visit. She is on her way from Israel to the States and decides to drop by to see him. I have the strong feeling that a key reason for her visit is to check me out and report back to the family. Later that month, Howard has to leave to participate in a retreat. Twice a year, in June and in December, there is a religious retreat for the Jewish troops in Europe. It is held in Berchtesgaden, in the mountains of Bavaria. That is in the south of Germany where Hitler built his home, the Eagle's Nest. Now, the town is host to hundreds of Jewish-American soldiers coming together for social and religious events. Talk about poetic justice! All Jewish chaplains stationed in Europe attend and participate. Howard takes off with Ceil as his guest. I am to follow in a few days, as I am still going to school. Ceil's presence calms my parents' doubts about my trip. We are to room together; she is to be my chaperone.

For me, the world disappears the moment Howard leaves town. I cannot sit still; I cannot study. I wander around the house like a captive bird whose wings have been clipped. There is no purpose in my life anymore. I feel empty and useless. That is when I realize how much I have become part of this man whom I have known for barely three months. Nothing—neither parents nor school nor friends—matter to me anymore. My noted "cool head" and the clear and logical thinking I always brag about have disappeared. When Howard calls a few days later, my hands and knees are shaking so that I barely hold on to the phone. My heart is beating as if it wants to tear my ribs apart.

There is no doubt in my mind that I am hooked for good, but I am still not really sure of his intentions. Is he playing with my feelings? The answer comes when I join him in Berchtesgaden. First, there is a dance for the soldiers. As

I love to dance and Howard does not, I have a great time doing the waltz, foxtrot, and tango with any willing GI. We are all sitting together around a big table, laughing, talking, and having a great time, when one of the young men with whom I was just dancing raises his glass and yells, "A toast to Mrs. Graber." There is a sudden silence. I do not know how to react, but Howard says calmly, "She is not my wife, but she will be." Later that evening, he declares, "We are going to get married." I am trying to decide, is this a proposal? I assume it is.

Of course, I had liked him when we first met. I cannot even say why or what specifically—looks, character or behavior—attracted me to him. And, of course, I was madly in love after our first date. There was nothing unusual about that. Teenagers —and I am just nineteen—are known to fall in love very quickly. The incredible thing is that he kept asking me for a date again and again. Within one month, I was completely under his spell. I could not study; I could not think; I could not sleep. I lived from one date to another. Where were my high hopes of becoming a famous psychologist? Where were my plans for a great career? Even the extensive summer trips I had so desperately longed for had no appeal anymore. I was starting to wonder where all this is going to end. Was my love just a teenager's big flame, which would surely die out; or was it the slow, durable fire that could last a lifetime?

Saturday, December 5. I wake up thinking, tomorrow I am getting married! Tomorrow! I am getting married! I, Felicia Bialecki. I am getting married! I still cannot believe it. I, who always seem to be the little wallflower. I, who has neither talent nor beauty. I am getting married. And not to just anybody, either. I am becoming the wife of a man whose name alone is enough to make every girl's heart beat faster. He is the most desirable Jewish bachelor in town.

Pangs of sorrow and fear grip my chest—sorrow for the beautiful months that lay behind us, filled with anticipation, excitement, and trips. Fear for the future. I shudder at the thought that this is the last day of innocence, independence, and irresponsibility. What does the future hold for me, for us? Will our overpowering passion lead toward mutual understanding and calm, durable love? Or will it just disappear once our thirst for each other is satisfied? Have I acted too quickly? Should I have waited before committing myself?

I suddenly realize that I am binding myself to Howard for as long as I live. I am walking through a door that will close behind me forever. This is not a childish whim. I can't say, "I am sorry," and pretend nothing happened if it does not work out. There is no return to how life used to be.

I panic. I cannot go through with it. I have to cancel the wedding, go into hiding, disappear. But, no, I cannot do that, either. Life is not a game. There is only one thing I can do—pray—and I do. *Please, God, help me. Help me on my way towards life. Help me to make my husband happy, to understand and support him. Help me to deserve the trust he has in me. And, most of all, Lord, give me the courage and strength to be a faithful and loyal wife, to stand steadfastly by him in good and evil, whether the sun shines on us or the storm smashes through our lives. In short, God, help me to be a good wife.*

December 6. We are married in the American Military Chapel. The ceremony is conducted by Major George Voda, the senior Jewish chaplain in Germany, and *Landesrabbiner* Dr. I.E. Lichtigfeld, the Chief Rabbi of Germany. The five-hundred-plus guests who pack the chapel consist of army chaplains, high-ranking officers, members of the Frankfurt Jewish community, Jewish army personnel, and American State Department employees. Following the ceremony and a short reception, about two hundred guests drive across town to a hall where the first post-war kosher wedding dinner in Frankfurt is served.

I do not find it difficult at all to change my life so drastically. It feels quite natural. I also don't believe that I am marrying an Orthodox man to prove to my parents that I am a "good girl" as some of my friends will later suggest. In fact, my mother and father are very worried that, in the long run, I will not be able to keep the obligation to this stringent lifestyle . They are afraid that I am too young, too inexperienced to know what I am getting myself into, that my emotions are overshadowing everything else. They are right. My feelings are pushing all rational thinking away, but I am determined. They are mistaken about the strength of my commitment. It is one I will keep for the rest of my life.

To say that a new life starts for me in more ways than I can count would be an understatement. I instantly become "the first lady" of an army congregation consisting of hundreds of soldiers, officers, and U.S. State Department employees and their families. Adjusting to my new religious lifestyle was a piece of cake compared to the demands on me now. I am expected to smile, greet, and make small talk with everyone

before and after services. After *Rosh Hashanah* services the
following year, Howard and I shake over five hundred hands,
and my mouth hurts from smiling. I have to join other chaplains' and officers' wives clubs for their monthly teas. One big
honor I receive is being asked to pour the tea at the general's
wife's reception for her "girls."

Whatever I do and whatever I wear becomes the subject
of gossip and sometimes criticism among the Jewish personnel and their wives. I am expected to attend the monthly
Jewish Chapel Sisterhood meetings and am asked to give
the invocation. I have to adapt to a new culture, new ways,
and new customs. The fact that Howard is very popular and
many Jewish officers' wives are happy that he has found a
"nice Jewish girl" helps a lot. Most congregants are very nice
to me, and I never feel that I am unfairly put upon. I believe
all this is just part of the whole package. I have married a
man who has an important job to do, and it is my duty to
help him. In fact, I see my priority as being Howard's support system, and I never resent it even if I do not enjoy my
"duties."

One of the problems I have to deal with early on is my
mother-in-law, who has come for the wedding and is staying
with us for a few weeks. She and I do not hit it off very well.
She has heard of the wheeling, dealing, and smuggling going
on by the survivors in the civilian population of post-war
Germany. She does not understand that some of it is a survival strategy for people who need to get back on their feet
after having lost not only all their material possessions but
also parents, wives, husbands, children, aunts, uncles, and
cousins. These people are desperate to restart their lives, and

some of them are willing to use almost any means to achieve that goal.

My mother-in-law feels that I am a foreigner who has snatched her only son, the apple of her eye. I don't even have a college degree, a minimum requirement as far as she is concerned. Somehow, we manage to make it until she returns to the States.

Spring 1960. Before the wedding, I had promised my father that I would continue my studies at the university after I get married. Now, I break that promise. I quit school because I have more important and enjoyable plans. Howard is assigned to participate in the dedication of American military cemeteries in Holland, Belgium, Luxemburg, and France. I refuse to stay home and study; I am determined to go with him. This trip is a very moving experience. We shake hands with Queen Juliana of Holland, the Grand Duke of Luxembourg, and King Baudoin of Belgium.

Our first stop is outside Luxembourg City where the cemetery is officially dedicated on July 4, 1960. Between three and four hundred people are gathered in an unusual atmosphere for such a large crowd. There is total silence. The silence seems to overpower everyone. People are sitting soundlessly and motionless. It is as if a spell has been cast over them, a spell so forceful that no one dares to whisper. Even nature is stock-still. No birds sing. The only sound comes from the hundreds of American and Luxembourg flags fluttering gently in the soft breeze. Behind us, a carpet of green grass stretches as far as the eye can see. It is dotted by rows and rows of symmetrically arranged white marble crosses and Stars of David in perfect military formation. It brings home how many young men sacrificed their lives to liberate us and save what was left of European Jewry.

Even before we were married, Howard tried to convince me that, as a chaplain and chaplain's wife, just as with a rabbi in a congregation, we cannot have any true friendships. I do not believe him. Some of the women, mostly American army doctors' wives, are so nice, taking me under their wings, that I refuse to think they are not my best friends. Well, I learn a hard lesson.

One of the ladies is especially nice to me. She tells me that she considers me her "little sister." She advises me during my pregnancy. After our daughter Sarah is born in December 1961, this lady holds a New Year's Eve party for us, and the following March she organizes a twenty-first birthday party for me.

Soon afterwards, however, this wonderful friendship comes to an abrupt end. My friend does not approve of one woman who regularly attends services on Friday nights. She feels strongly that this person is just trying to take advantage of some lonely soldier and land herself an American husband. She demands that Howard bar the woman from the chapel. Howard cannot do that, of course. The chapel is a public place open to everyone. It is not a private institution, and the woman's behavior does not violate any norms. When my friend realizes that her wishes will not be heeded, she never speaks to either of us again. This type of situation repeats itself several times, and I soon learn that there is a definite barrier between the congregants and us—a barrier, which I learn over time, is a fact of life among clergy of all faiths. Luckily, there are a few exceptions. One couple and their three young daughters become true, good friends. He works for the Central Intelligence Agency, as we find out years later, and she becomes my model of an American Jewish woman. She teaches me how to bake some typical American desserts —jelly rolls and angel food cake—and she instructs me in many other Jewish-American customs, which make my transition into the American way of life easier.

December 18, 1961. Our daughter, Sarah Rachelle, is born in the American military hospital in Frankfurt. I come home two days after Sarah's birth and am almost immediately inundated with visitors and well wishers from the military community. As much as I appreciate their concern and caring, I am overwhelmed, as well as exhausted. I am also anxious that Howard's routine not be disturbed. I am a typical, old-fashioned wife during those years; my husband's comfort and needs are of utmost importance to me.

The first Friday night after I come home from the hospital with Sarah, I become distraught when she starts crying in the middle of our dinner. In my foolish young mind, I am concerned that Howard might be disturbed if his dinner is interrupted. Of course, he never expresses any such thoughts. It probably never even enters his mind. It is just my intense desire for him to have all my attention that causes me trouble.

August 8, 1963. Twenty months later, our son Steven is

born, and by the end of the year, Howard receives his orders
to be reassigned to the States. I finally realize my dream to
move to America, except that, now, I am not really so anxious to go. I have my family and my parents here in Frankfurt. I have become adjusted to my roles as chaplain's wife
and a mother, and I am enjoying my life. The fact that I am
still in Germany is a moot point right now, because I live and
socialize only with the American community.

Friday evening, November 22. Howard has left for the
chapel to conduct services. I am sitting and reading, as we
do not watch television on *Shabbat*, when I hear a knock on
the door. My next-door neighbor is there, looking terribly
upset, and says, "Felicia, did you hear? President Kennedy
has been shot!" We are both incredulous, do not know what
to do, and feel helpless. There is really nothing we can do but
listen and watch the news. When Howard comes home later
that evening, he tells me that he had heard about the shooting when he got to the chapel and immediately conducted
special prayers for the president as people started to stream in
to pray. Nobody really cared that this was a Jewish religious
service. People needed to find some solace in a house of God.
These are very upsetting days for everyone. The day the army
sends the movers to pack our things, I sit in front of the television, watching President Kennedy's funeral.

Howard pulls some strings and gets the army to send us
home on the SS United States. We are to leave on December
16, and we look forward to five days of a leisurely vacation
on board. Well, things do not quite work out that way. First

of all, two-year-old Sarah has not yet recovered from a bad ear infection on the day of our departure from Frankfurt. She is still running a fever and is on antibiotics. We take the overnight train to Le Havre to board the ship, but, during the trip, we are informed that the ship has been delayed coming from the States because of a very big storm in the Atlantic. We are told to get out of the train in Paris in the early morning and wait there until evening when we will catch the evening train for Le Havre.

Well, I do love Paris. Under different circumstances I would be delighted to have a free day here, but not with a four-month-old baby and a sick two-year-old in the middle of winter. When we arrive in Paris, it is freezing and pouring rain. How can we wait in the cold, drafty train station all day with a sick child? Howard comes to the rescue. He finds us a hotel where we get something to eat, warm up, and relax in comfortable beds. That evening, we go back to the train station and finally board the ship at two a.m. on December 18. It is Sarah's second birthday.

Our hopes for five nice vacation days are dampened when we find out that the shipping company has discontinued the kosher kitchen, and we have to make do with frozen TV dinners. In the end, this does not matter much because the sea is very rough all the way to the States, and Howard spends most days sick in bed. I am also worried about Steven, who sleeps all day long. I can hardly wake him up to feed him. The ship's doctor reassures me, however, that he is fine; he is just being rocked to sleep by the ship. Sarah is much better and very happy to play in the ship's playroom.

Christmas Eve 1963. We arrive in New York Harbor during one of the biggest snowstorms in the city's history.

Chapter 11: 1963 to 1965
Mount Vernon, Fort Hamilton, & Fort Bragg, United States

December 24, 1963. We are met by Howard's mother and sister and a few other members of the family, all of whom braved the horrible snowstorm in order to welcome us. My great-aunt Lina has come, as well, so that someone from "my family" would be represented. I want to tell her how grateful I am for her presence, but as soon as we clear customs, the children and I are rushed into a car and driven away. Howard stays behind to take care of the luggage and follows with his sister, Connie. On the way to Westchester, where the family lives, I am informed that we will be staying with Howard's mother, Dorothy, rather than with his sister, as we had expected. Dorothy lives in a two-bedroom apartment with her twin sister, Lil, and Lil's husband, Harry. I am not happy about this turn of events, but there is nothing I can do.

Before we met, Howard had decided to make the army his career, and I was fully aware of that. Now, he has to spend six months at the chaplains' school in Fort Hamilton, New York, to take the advanced chaplain course. Classes will start after the New Year, so we cannot move into our quarters until then.

Before we left Frankfurt, Howard and I had discussed where we would stay while we waited for our quarters. In the meantime, I wanted to go to a hotel, since the army would put us up until we could move into our new apartment on base. But Howard was reluctant to hurt his family's feelings, so he accepted Connie's invitation.

Now, in New York, I find out that the plans have been changed. We will stay with Dorothy, who gives up her room and plans to sleep on the couch in the living room. This is hardly what I would have chosen.

To make matters even more uncomfortable, my curious, inquisitive Sarah decides to make herself at home as soon as we arrive at the apartment by opening every drawer and closet door to investigate what is inside. Before I have a chance to stop her, she pulls everything out.

Somehow, the couple of weeks or so go by without too many problems. Connie turns out to be as nice as I expected. She does whatever she can to make me feel at home. Another wonderful person is Howard's cousin, Rita. She gives us a beautiful welcoming party and invites Howard's entire, large family. As Howard is everyone's favorite, all I hear all evening is "how lucky" I am to have Howard as my husband. Finally, Rita chimes in, "Howard is also a lucky one to have met Felicia." I will never forget Rita's warm words.

We finally move into our own apartment in Fort Hamilton, Brooklyn, New York. I do not mind that it is tiny; I am just happy to have my own place. However, the months here turn out to be very lonely ones for me. We live on the fifth floor of a high-rise. Howard is very busy with his classes. He is hardly ever home, and, when he is, he must study and do homework. I am alone with the two little ones, and even everyday chores become complicated. For example, doing laundry turns into a strategic undertaking. The washing machines and dryers are in the basement. How do I take two small children and the laundry basket down from the fifth floor? Well, I put the five-month-old in the playpen in his infant seat, with the television turned on to entertain him, take the two-year-old in one hand and the laundry basket in the other, and go. Somehow, it works.

Here we are in the middle of Brooklyn, a city with millions of Jews, but we are the only Jews in our huge complex. The other tenants are all officers' and chaplains' families. I have very little in common with the wives and do not fit in. For a few weeks, the chaplains' wives are asked to attend a class in which we learn what to do or not to do and how to behave in conjunction with our status: "Never discuss your husband with the congregants," we are told. "When referring to him, never use his first name. Rather, use his title or 'my husband.' Remember, you are a model for other wives and mothers, as well as surrogate mothers to the single boys. How do you feel about these duties as a clergy's wife? Do you resent or enjoy them? How do you see your role?" ... and so on and so on.

One afternoon, in desperation and loneliness, I take the kids and venture out of the army compound to drive to see Sylvia Brand, my father's cousin's wife, who lives in Flatbush. I am terrified to drive in New York and almost collide with another car at a major intersection. A friendly police officer approaches my car to make sure everyone is okay. He means well, but I am intimidated, as I am still not comfortable around officials in uniform.

Sunday afternoons mean mandatory trips to Connie's house where the family gets together. I have no say in what we are doing. We just go. I cannot wait for Howard to be transferred out of New York. The matriarchs of the family— Dorothy, Lil, and their older sister, Hen—are very competitive. I am constantly reminded of how smart, beautiful, and talented one of Howard's cousins is. Right or wrong, I take it as personal criticism.

Sarah is pressured to compete with her two contemporary little cousins. "You mean, you cannot write your name yet? Howard, how come she cannot write her name yet? Her two cousins can." I have a hard time keeping my mouth shut and seldom succeed, which does not make me popular with the family. I admire Connie, who takes everything in stride, smiles, nods, and does as she pleases. Nothing seems to faze her. She always manages to stay above the fray and to keep her daughter away from the competition.

June 1963. We finally receive our orders to move to Fort

Aunt Rachel Kresch and paternal grandparents,
Sarah and Leib Israel Lederberger

Maternal grandmother

My mother,
Tosia Lederberger

My father,
Salomon Lederberger

Felicia 1941

Felicia 1945

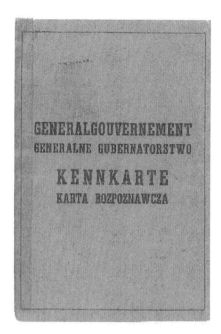

Cover of false identification papers

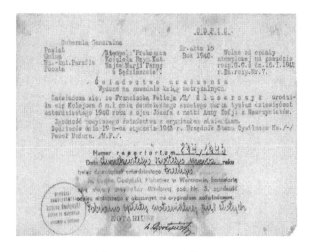

Notorized copy of my
forged birth certificate

Father's forged Aryan identification document. Notice different last name from mother's.

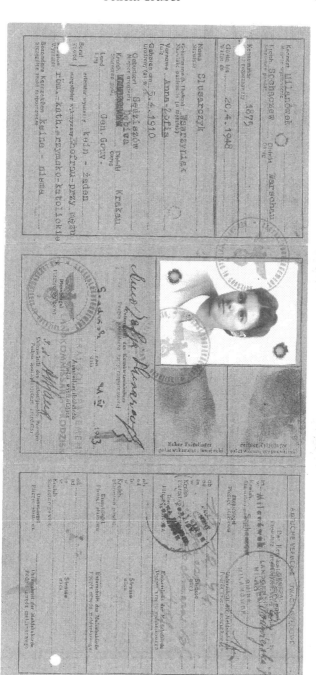

Mother's forged Aryan identification document

Piotr and Eleanore Sierocinki, Polish farmer and his wife who provided shelter to our family from October 1944 until after Liberation

On Sopot Pier 1945

With Tommy 1946

Our Wedding, December 6, 1959

Tarnow Cemetery in 1994

Memorial in Buszyna Forest erected in memory of thousands of Jews
shot here on June 11, 1942

Bimah (altar) remains of the
Grand Tarnow synagogue burned by the Germans in 1939

Maternal Grandmother's grave before and after restoration

With Janina and Wladzia, the Sierocinki sisters, in 1994

With Howard, in 2005

Bragg, North Carolina. I am thrilled. The army provides us with a beautiful, three-bedroom house. I have never lived in a single-family house, and I love it. Also, as help is cheap here in the South, I am able to hire a woman to come in once a week. She is wonderful with the children, which is most important to me, because the moment she walks in, I walk out. Whatever housework she gets done is icing on the cake. I get a few hours to myself.

Being a chaplain's wife here in the States is different from being one in Germany. The soldiers go home for the Jewish Holy Days, so we have our own private celebrations, as well as our own Passover Seder for the first time. We still have GIs over for Friday-night dinners and Shabbat lunches as we did in Frankfurt. We are temporary family for these young men. At this time, the military draft exempts women, so there are few women in the congregation, except for the officers' families. My duties here are easier than in Germany. There is a small sisterhood. I teach Sunday school, but there is relatively little pressure.

Life would be great except for my feelings of incompetence and inadequacy. When Howard comes home, he tells me about the intelligent, well-educated women who come for "counseling," to discuss their problems with the chaplain. I cringe. I cannot compete with those bright, sophisticated Americans. I feel like a little lost country girl. It seems that all I am capable of discussing are diapers, formulas, and feeding issues. I know I have to do something about it, both for my sanity and my self-esteem.

Although Howard never indicates that I might not be adequate, I take all his remarks very personally. So, when the University of North Carolina opens a branch on base, I quickly enroll in a course and am both in heaven and purgatory. I love the intellectual challenge and the one night a week off, but I am like a blind woman feeling my way into the foreign, American college scene. It is so different from the "do as you will" attitude of the German university system. I am scared stiff of the final exam; we never had any in Frankfurt. I just know that I will fail.

On the day of the exam, I arrive at class, almost trembling; and, to my great shock, I see my name along with a few others on the blackboard. What does that mean? Why is my name up there? What did I do wrong? Finally, the teacher walks in and announces, "If your name is on the board, you are excused from the final. You already have an A in the class and can go home." I blurt out, "You must be kidding!" "Oh no," he says "I am dead serious. You are excused." Talk about a morale booster!

Everything is going relatively well until April 1965, when President Johnson decides to send 30,000 paratroopers and marines to the Dominican Republic to quash a revolt by the local army. Howard is attached to the 115th hospital unit of the 82nd Airborne Division, one of the elite forces dispatched to the Caribbean. About two a.m. one morning, he gets a phone call to report for duty. These duty alarms take place about once a month, but this call is not an alarm he is told. He is being shipped out. I am devastated. I do not know what to do. Soon, the only men in the camp are pediatricians and gynecologists.

Rumors spread like wildfire: "The men are being shipped to Vietnam. They are being held at the nearby Air Force base.

They are going to the Dominican Republic. They are not allowed to contact anyone. Their location is a state secret. Watch out; young men from Fayetteville are prowling the fort, knowing that the women are left all alone. The military police are patrolling, but you need to be careful."

Now, more than forty years later, I still recall how I felt that spring morning. I stand and wave good-bye until Howard's car disappears. The ensuing silence is frightening. I feel like I am having a bad dream. I cannot grasp that I am left alone. The thunder of Air Force troop carriers overhead brings me back to reality. I must stop feeling sorry for myself. I have to pull myself together. In just a few hours, the children will be up. I'd better get some sleep. He is not gone forever. Maybe they'll end this stupid revolution in a few days, and then we'll both laugh at the whole fuss.

Yet, after locking the door behind me, helplessness and loneliness overtake me. It is too quiet. The ticking of the living room clock is unbelievably loud; it makes the living room seem even emptier. Suddenly, I just have to talk to somebody. Anybody. Just talk. Talk the ache out of my system. But whom can I call at three-thirty in the morning? On an impulse, for want of any other means of communication, I take out a piece of paper and begin to write:

The rear lights of the car disappear. A second later, even the faint growl of the motor is engulfed by the silence of the night. I am brutally dumped into a cold, gloomy, isolated world. Bright stars stare down coldly, indifferent to my plight. Their light makes me shiver. The dark houses around me seem to be props, set up to create an eerie atmosphere for a detective story. Slowly, I turn toward the house, hoping to find some consolation within the familiar walls, some comfort in the cozy rooms. As I walk in, however, the light pouring out of the door seems just as indifferent and cold as the stars above. Like a sleepwalker, I cross the threshold and lock the door behind me.

What now? I look around, amazed to find the room intact, in the same condition it has been for months. I expected to see everything shattered and broken. I expected to find the house in the same turmoil in which I find myself. Yet, nothing has changed. The couch still shows the contours of his body. His socks lay on the floor. His empty coffee cup still stands on the end table. For a while, I remain standing still, my back against the door, numb, feeling like an abandoned child. I tear myself away from the door and try to decide what to do next.

I sit down on the sofa and attempt to collect myself. I am not a child anymore. I am supposed to be a mature woman; I am now in charge of our children. The whole burden rests on my shoulders until his return. I shudder, His return ... when will that be? In a day, in a month, or in a year? Will he come under fire? Oh God! What if he gets hit? Maybe that would help to bring him back? What thoughts. I am being childish. The atrocious reality of war hits me. Every single individual in those jungles has a home, a wife, children, and parents. Every soldier's death means a young life uselessly cut at its roots—a life that could make a contribution to the world; a life that would give his family support, comfort, and leadership.

"Mommy! Mommy!" I jump up, startled. I must have fallen asleep. Where am I? What am I doing on the couch? I run to help the baby out of the crib and then console my three-year-old, who is bewildered to find an empty bed when she comes for her daily morning cuddle. "Where is Daddy?" she wants to know, while I wipe her tears away. This innocent question pierces my heart. How do you tell a three-year-old that her father has gone to war? What do you tell her when she asks her usual "why"? I do not want to scare her, so I throw in a casual, "He had to go away for a while." Luckily, children have short memories and take things in stride. So, soon my two are back to their daily routine of playing, eating, and sleeping, in that order of importance.

How does a grown woman, though, who has been spoiled like a child, adjust to her new role as head of the family? How does she conceal her weakness, loneliness, and aches and lead a normal life? Things are not that easy. At every step, I encounter difficulties. I had never had any responsibilities outside of running the house. I do not even know how to write or endorse a check.

About a week or so after Howard leaves on that spring morning, I finally receive a letter from him. The good news: he is not in Vietnam; he is in the Dominican Republic. The not-so-good news: he is sleeping in a tent, on mud, with tarantulas crawling around him. He is not pleased with the way the army takes care of the men. He feels that the soldiers are made to fight with one hand tied behind their backs, that they are not given the full freedom and information to do the job. He attributes that as a lack of leadership.

As a chaplain, he is not allowed to carry a weapon but

is to be protected by his chaplain's assistant, Mike. I know Mike. He is always a favorite with the children when he visits our house, bringing doughnuts and other goodies. But, as large as Mike is, he is still only one man. When Howard's driver makes a wrong turn in the road, they end up near enemy territory, requiring them to hide behind a wall while shots fly from all sides. Luckily, help arrives quickly, and they get to safety unharmed. Shivers run down my back when he tells me this story. I realize that my fears have been realistic despite the common perception that chaplains never get in harm's way.

In the Dominican Republic, Howard serves troops from all religions and all armed services branches. He gets a helicopter ride to a troop carrier at sea. Two of his reports to the National Jewish Welfare Board are included in the United States Congress' Congressional Record. Then, about six weeks later—six weeks that seem like a lifetime to me—one morning, without warning, the doorbell rings; and he is standing in front me. Sarah describes this best: "I woke up, and Daddy was there, and we were not sad anymore."

Those six weeks have changed my life. They are the catalyst that transforms me from a porcelain doll, a submissive follower, a woman of the 1950s, into a woman of action, a woman who is able to stand on her own two feet. When Howard returns, he finds someone who has taken charge of her life. Eventually, I will get a college degree and, later, a teaching job. I will become a woman who can share in the shaping of her future, together with her husband; a woman who, in other words, becomes a Super Mom of the eighties and nineties.

When he returns, however, Howard is having second thoughts about his career in the army. We have known he would have to serve at least one year in Korea without us, his family; but, now, the specter of Vietnam becomes a dark reality. President Johnson keeps sending more and more troops to Southeast Asia.

One quiet Sunday afternoon, soon after his return, the telephone rings. A voice I don't recognize asks, "Can I talk to Rabbi Graber?" This simple question strikes me. I have never heard Howard referred to as "Rabbi," only as "Chaplain." Who is this person? When Howard gets off the phone, he tells me that it was the president of a small congregation in Iowa. He is looking for a rabbi, and someone has given him Howard's name. This news hits me like lightning. For me, this telephone call is a sign that reads, "Make a move. Leave the army." Suddenly, I realize that there are other options for us out there. We have to take it seriously and investigate the possibilities.

Howard goes to Iowa but comes back unsure that this could work out. Iowa is in the middle of the country with very little Jewish culture or educational opportunities for the children. He does not see any future for us there. But I am insistent, "Go to New York," I say. "Speak to Yeshiva University, to your yeshiva. I feel that the telephone call was a sign. We just have to leave the army."

Howard does go to New York. He consults with the Rabbinic Placement Department and others he respects. When he returns, he has decided that he is staying in. "It is a very competitive world out there," he reports, "I will never be able to make it. Here, in the army, I have a steady, secure paycheck. In twelve more years, I can retire and have a pension for life. I cannot give all this up.

But I argue, "I don't believe that you can't make it in the civilian world. A secure paycheck is not the only thing in life. There are other considerations. If Iowa is not suitable, let's look around. Surely, there are other congregations that are looking for a rabbi. I don't care where we go, but we must do it."

While I speak with conviction and certainty, I am terrified. What am I doing? What kind of responsibility am I taking? What if he doesn't make it? Then, what? What will happen in twelve years, when his retirement would have come due? Will he blame me for the decision to leave a secure income? I am not sure how I manage to be so certain and convinced, but I feel strongly that the phone call was a sign for us, that we must make this drastic move.

Through an ad in a Jewish periodical, Howard finds out that there is a congregation in the small town of Ellwood City, Pennsylvania, that is also looking for a rabbi. He goes there to interview. Now, synagogues in two different states want him badly. Iowa has a better salary and a bigger parsonage house, but it is in the middle of nowhere. Ellwood City is a smaller community with a smaller salary and smaller house, but it is fifty miles away from Pittsburgh where there is a large Jewish community. The University of Pittsburgh also has an Education department where Howard can fulfill his dream of going for a PhD in Jewish education. This would permit him to leave the rabbinate and devote his life to that field. I vote for Ellwood City. I feel it has more potential for our future.

After hours of discussion and reflection, Howard turns in his resignation to the Department of the Armed Forces and accepts the pulpit in Pennsylvania. In fall of 1965, we leave Fort Bragg and the army forever.

Chapter 12: 1965 to 1968
Ellwood City, Pennsylvania

Summer **1965.** We move into our new home in
Ellwood City. I have not seen it and am a little ap-
prehensive; but it is a nice, adequate, three-bedroom
ranch. My life changes again, of course. Now, I am no longer
a chaplain's wife; I am the *rebbetzin*—the rabbi's wife. Ellwood City is a small town where everyone knows everyone.
So, wherever I go, I am greeted with, "You must be the new
rabbi's wife. You don't look like a rabbi's wife." I am not sure
whether the latter is a compliment or not. I am not sure
what a rabbi's wife is supposed to look like, but I am not
about to ask that question. I have been well trained from
early childhood: you do not ask questions; you do not rock
the boat; you do not challenge anyone; you just accept what

is going on. So, I just smile and say, "Thank you."

A few days after we move in, I meet a neighbor who lives across the street. She tells me, "I need to tell you a cute story. My daughter, Annie, came home from school the other day with a new classmate. When I asked the little girl who she was, she told me, 'I am the new rabbi's daughter.' Isn't that cute?" Again, I smile and agree. "Cute."

Inside, however, I cringe, That is not what I want for my children. I do not want them to be identified by their father's position in a community. I want them to be identified as who they are. I am not comfortable with the situation, but, again, I do not say anything. This is all part of my life. I am happy that we are out of the army, that Howard will not be sent to Korea or Vietnam. I will make the best of it.

Howard is very popular with the congregants. Everyone loves him. I, too, feel accepted. I do what I can to be a good *rebetzin*. I become the chaplain of the sisterhood, give invocations before meetings, attend all synagogue functions, go to services every week, and am present at all *bar* and *bat mitzvah* celebrations, baby namings, and communal events.

I also try to further my education and pursue some of my own interests. Howard receives a grant from the GI Bill to go back to school. He enrolls in a PhD program at the University of Pittsburgh. Since it is a state school, there is enough money for both of us to attend. I hire a baby sitter for Monday afternoons and evenings; and, once a week, Howard and I drive from Ellwood City to Pittsburgh to go to classes.

I hope to earn a Bachelor of Arts (BA) eventually, but, since I cannot handle more than one class per semester, I am not sure whether it is feasible. I still struggle with the American college system, where the teachers assume that you went through the US schools and take many things for granted. They assume that we all have been taught how to write a research paper and how to handle footnotes. They assume that all of us had read Mark Twain, for example, and are familiar with his life and travels. I have never read Twain, know nothing about his life, have never written a research paper, a bibliography, or footnotes.

Somehow, I muddle through the classes successfully. As I don't know if I will ever manage to get a degree, I do not declare a major and just take classes in the areas I enjoy: political science, history, literature, and writing.

Summer 1967. I hire the daughter of a friend from Pittsburgh. She gets to spend ten weeks in a rural area with free room and board, far from the Pittsburgh's smog. In exchange, she watches my children a few hours a day. I intend to use my free time to write, but I have no direction, no specific goal, I cannot think of anything to write, so I accomplish nothing.

That year, Elie Wiesel's book, *Night*, becomes a best seller. I am mesmerized by this book and his other two autobiographical novels, *Dawn* and *The Accident*. I decide that I must give a book report on *Night* to the synagogue sisterhood. I convince Howard to drop a hint to the president of the group, and I am invited to give that talk. The problem? I have never given a book report before. I have no idea where to start or how to go about it. I just know that I have to do it. I sweat it out and do manage to speak for about thirty minutes. I guess I don't do such a great job because I am never asked to speak again.

1967 is an important year in my life. It is the year I become an American citizen. From the time we left Poland in 1947 until now, I have been a stateless person—a person without citizenship. Whenever and wherever I traveled in Europe, it was a great hassle. I was considered an alien everywhere. I needed a visa to enter every country, even if I just wanted to pass through for a few kilometers. I did not have the protection of any government or a country to call my own.

The reason I never accompanied Howard when he had to travel to Berlin on army business was that I was afraid to travel through the Russian Zone. I was scared the Communists might detain me, as I was a refugee from their regime in Poland. I could not count on any government to stand by me or to receive assistance from any authority.

While we were still living in Germany, Howard and I traveled quite a bit. I had to apply for an entry visa for every country we went to. This usually took between two and six weeks. Once we were driving to Italy and wanted to take a shortcut through Switzerland for a few kilometers. The Swiss border patrol told Howard that he could go but would not let me through. There was no European Union then, and individual countries guarded their borders jealously. They were terrified that some renegade, stateless individual might (God forbid) try to overstay his or her welcome.

Now, in 1967, as the spouse of an American, I am able to apply for citizenship within three years of my arrival, instead of the customary five. Still, there is a lot of paper work involved. I need to produce a birth certificate, my alien registration card, and my marriage certificate. I need witnesses to swear that I am an upstanding and honest person, and I need to take a test. I study, pass, get all the paperwork together; and the big day arrives. It is a dream come true. I finally belong somewhere. I have a country to call my own.

I am happy in Ellwood City. Everyone in this small American town is very friendly and treats us like VIPs. What I do not like is living in a "glass house." Everything Howard, I, or the children do is discussed and is food for gossip. When Howard disciplines our daughter, Sarah, in Hebrew school, I get a call from a congregant saying that her daughter was upset that the rabbi got angry at his daughter for misbehaving. "Please, tell the Rabbi to do his disciplining at home," she says. Steven, our son, is very sensitive to the unwanted attention he generates. When he is dressed in a new outfit for the Holy Days and congregants surround him, saying, "Oh, how cute," he gets very upset, thinking that they are making fun of him. He is self-conscious and dislikes being the center of all that attention.

One of my big challenges during these three years is raising our children in a traditional Jewish lifestyle. We are the only *Shabbat*-observant family in town. I have to improvise to make the *Shabbat* special for the children. They do not have friends to play with who are in the same situation. They cannot watch television on that day and have many other restrictions on activities they enjoy. In order to counter that, I give them each a "*Shabbat* treat" every week. It is nothing expensive—a little one-or-two-dollar toy—but it is enough to make the day special for them. They truly look forward to that day, wondering what each week's surprise will be.

Howard works very hard. Besides his rabbinic duties, like conducting services and giving sermons every week, he teaches Sunday school and Hebrew school three times a week. He conducts programs for adults and children of the congregation, acts as the Jewish representative to the Christian community, takes on a part-time job teaching once a week at Slippery Rock College, and studies towards his PhD. As a result, many of our children's daily religious activities depend on me. I, who had hardly any Jewish education, learn some prayers, teach them, and recite them with the children every night. I want to make sure they do not fall behind in their Jewish knowledge and that they incorporate Judaism into their daily lives.

It helps that Sarah's first grade teacher is very sensitive to her students' needs. Sarah is the only Jewish child in class, but before Christmas the teacher makes a billboard, divides it in half—one half for Chanukah and one half for Christmas. Every day of Chanukah Sarah is asked to post an additional cardboard "flame" on the billboard's menorah. I am grateful. Yet, it is a challenge to raise children the way I would like to in this environment. I hope for a day when we can move to a place that has a Jewish day school where our children will receive the education necessary to live traditional Jewish lives and can have friends with similar backgrounds.

Well, my wish does come true. Howard's advisor at the University of Pittsburgh offers him a job in that city as the director of the School of Advanced Jewish Studies. We are thrilled. That is exactly what we had hoped would happen when we moved to Ellwood City. We will be moving to a city with a strong Jewish population and a Jewish day school for our children, and I will no longer be a *rebetzin*. Life is getting better and better.

Howard hands in his resignation to the board of the synagogue, and everyone is dutifully sorry to see us leave. As much as I have enjoyed living in this small town, I am very excited and look forward to our new life. Of course, everything in life has its pros and cons. Now that we are no longer a rabbinic family, there are no more "perks," like free parsonage housing, a congregation to pay for our move, or free dental or medical care supplied by members of the community. We move from being totally cared for by the army, then partially supported by the congregation, to being completely on our own, without any outside support system.

Still, I am delighted. I feel liberated, again. No more duties, no more living in a glass house, no more worrying about what I wear or what my children and I do. I am free.

Chapter 13: 1968 to 1972
Pittsburgh, Pennsylvania

Fall 1968. We rent a nice three-bedroom apartment in Pittsburgh. Our landlady, who lives upstairs, is very stern and heavy-handed. Even though she lives above us and cannot possibly hear footsteps, she demands that the children wear slippers when they are home because their running in the house disturbs her. When the Festival of *Sukkoth* (the Feast of Tabernacles) comes in the fall, Steven is thrilled that we will have our own *Sukkah* (a traditional hut), a temporary dwelling that Jews use during this holiday. He bursts out to our landlady, "We are having our own *Sukkah*."

Well, our landlady is not amused. "Not on my property you aren't," she says. "Oh, yes, we are," claims my excited five-year old. She knocks on our door and tells me, "There will be no booth on my property." I decide to leave the matter up to the "rabbi." His title carries much more weight than a mere Mrs. Graber. Howard manages to soothe our landlady and gets her to agree to have a booth ... but only at the back of the house so that it is not visible from the street.

Both children are enrolled in Hillel Academy, the local Jewish day school. I feel relieved that the burden of their Jewish education has been taken from my shoulders and that I no longer have duties related to Howard's work. Even though he is still a community leader, there are no demands on me. I still must be careful about what I say and to whom I say it because of his position in the community, but I have been well trained for that since my childhood.

Now, I seriously begin to consider working toward a college degree. I have some credits accumulated from Fort Bragg, as well as from Pittsburgh, but far from enough unless I can get my courses accepted from the year and a half I spent at the university in Frankfurt. This is a major problem. The German university system is totally different from the American one. In Germany, for the first few years, there are lectures but no tests. Students sign up for classes, attend lectures, and have the professors verify that they attended. That is all that is needed. Eventually, when the students feel ready, they take a major test that covers all the material necessary to prove that they are knowledgeable in their fields. If they pass this test, they receive their degrees and are admitted to their professions.

Since I never reached the testing stage, all I have is a booklet that only lists courses signed by my teachers. This means nothing to American college administrators. They do not understand that kind of system and are not willing or able to give me any college credit for those eighteen months. I investigate my options and am told repeatedly that I have no chance of receiving any American college credits based on this evidence.

Encouraged by Howard, I try again. I go to see the dean of General Studies of the University of Pittsburgh's evening, adult-education school, where I am enrolled. I show him what I have and explain the situation. To my great surprise, he does not dismiss me. He examines my current American transcripts and advises me, "Translate the names of the courses you have in your booklet, get a University of Pittsburgh catalogue, pick which of our courses are roughly equivalent to the ones you took, and match them up. I will send all that information to the Department of Education in Washington D.C. If the Department okays it, we will be able to give you up to seventy credits. There is one caveat, however. You will receive these credits only after you complete all other courses and earn the additional credits required for a BA from our school."

I am thrilled. A degree has become a real possibility. I do everything he suggests and turn it all over to the dean. To my great delight, the plan works. Washington approves the courses from Frankfurt, and the following year, when both children are in school all day, I enroll as a full-time student. It is not easy. Between the work load, the house, and the children, I struggle. Howard works long hours. He recruits students, administers the school during the day, teaches every evening, and works on his PhD.

Summer 1969. I enroll the children in day camp and take three classes. In addition, I use my knowledge of French and German to earn additional credits by taking advance placement tests. The following year, 1970, I have only two courses left to finish my BA in social sciences, a degree which is useful only "to sell ties at a street corner," as my advisor informs me. With all the history, sociology, psychology, and political courses under my belt, that is the fastest way for a BA; and a degree is a degree, however useless it may be.

Howard continues his administrative work, his teaching, and his studies. In addition, he takes on a part-time rabbinical job at Parkway Jewish Center in a small community near Pittsburgh where he conducts services once a month. Although this job requires nothing of me, it affects the family, as Howard is away from home one Shabbat a month.

May 4, 1970. The Kent State shooting. Aside from the horror of the event, Howard receives a call that one of the victims is nineteen-year old Allison Krause, the daughter of a member of the Parkway Jewish Center. He is asked to officiate at her funeral, a task he would rather not have to perform.

He also takes on jobs in small communities in Pennsylvania and West Virginia for the High Holy Days. These small congregations do not have the funds for a full-time rabbi, so they hire one only for the three days a year—the two days of *Rosh Hashanah*, the Jewish New Year, and *Yom Kippur*, the Day of Atonement. This means that we have to pack up and spend these Holy Days, either as guests in someone's home or sleeping on cots in the synagogue. We usually have to bring our own food along, as there are very few people in those towns who observe *kashrus* (the Jewish dietary laws). I am not thrilled with this, of course. I would rather observe the Holy Days at home and have our son sit with his father during these important services. But I know that the extra income is vital for us.

In the meantime, I convince Howard that I should try to get a part-time job. At first, he is very reluctant to even discuss the issue. His first reaction is, "No wife of mine is going to work." He is an old-fashioned husband; he married a woman who was an old-fashioned wife.

Now, things are changing, I am not the woman he married—the wife whose goal in life was to please her husband and be his support system. Now, I demand a life, a career of my own. I am no longer content to be in the background. The women's movement is having an effect on me. I want to become a liberated American woman—one who earns her husband's respect—not a dependent little "mouse." My poor husband does not know what is happening. I have to give him credit, though. He puts up with this change, manages to handle the situation, and is able to adjust to the new kind of person I have become.

Once Howard gets used to the new me, he is very supportive. He suggests that I go to the Pittsburgh Board of Education and apply to teach French and German. I have never been in charge of a classroom, have never taught anything but a few Sunday school classes to five-year-olds, but I go to investigate the possibilities. The foreign-language coordinator, a native German, interviews me. She speaks to me in German for a few minutes and realizes that I really do know the language. As this is the Vietnam War era, teachers are hard to find, especially those who speak a foreign language and who have most of the required credits for a college degree. She puts me on the substitute list as a German and French teacher, and I enroll for my last two college classes.

Spring 1970. I receive a call. It seems that a German teacher has had a car accident and will be out of commission for the last six weeks of the year. I am asked to take over for her. She is an itinerant teacher who teaches grades two through nine in three different schools. I accept the offer and, somehow, survive those six weeks. In fact, I must do something right because in the fall, I am offered a permanent, part-time position at Latimer Junior High School in the city. I am given an emergency teaching certificate under the condition that I return to school and become certified.

Latimer is an inner-city school with a very mixed student population. The principal, Mr. Bellini, is a strict, tough, but fair man who maintains control of the students. When all the schools in the area are forced to close because of racial rioting, Mr. Bellini manages to keep Latimer open with the help of extra security guards. I teach three German classes and enroll in Duquesne University in a Master of Arts in Teaching program, which allows a university supervisor to come and observe me at Latimer. This replaces practice teaching, so I do not have to quit my job and be assigned a non-paying, student-teaching position.

Somehow, I juggle home, kids, work, and school. One consequence from this period of my life comes to light years later. Once a week, when I have classes in the evening, I stick a frozen turkey breast in the oven for Howard and the children before leaving for school. Many years later, Steven, now a married man with children of his own, reacts when the subject of the turkey comes up. "I dreaded that turkey, and I hate turkey to this day," he says. "It reminds me of those days." That shows that one never knows what affects one's children. I do not know whether it was the meal or the fact that I was leaving that created this reaction.

Back in Pittsburgh, at Latimer, I run into problems with my supervisor on the Board of Education. She comes to observe me and scolds me in front of the class, saying that I cannot maintain discipline, do not have a good lesson plan, and do not know how to teach. Literally in tears, I go to see Mr. Bellini after school and learn that she had stomped into his office and demanded that he fire me. "I will do no such thing," he tells me. "We need you. You are a nice person. You will, at least, cause no harm. Teachers are either born or made. You belong to the second group. I am confident that you will become an excellent teacher. You just need more experience. With my luck, once you become good, you will leave to go somewhere else." It turns out that his words are prophetic.

I receive my Master of Arts in Teaching and teacher certification in the spring of 1972, and we leave Pittsburgh that summer to move to St Louis. I hate leaving Pittsburgh. I have made a few very good friends, the children are well adjusted, and we just bought our first house the year before. But the St Louis job is a very good opportunity for Howard. He is to establish a Jewish afternoon high school and become its principal and teacher. There is also the strong possibility that Howard will be able to take over the newly established Central Agency for Jewish Education, as its director plans to retire in a couple of years.

This is exactly what Howard wants. That is his goal, so we cannot let the opportunity slip away. We decide to move.

Chapter 14: 1972 to 1986
St. Louis, Missouri

Memorial Day Weekend 1972. It is a Saturday. We are in St. Louis looking at houses, either to rent or buy. As my brother lives here, and he and his wife are out of town, we are staying in their apartment. It is right next door to an Orthodox synagogue, but that is not the one where we want to attend services. We decide to walk to another synagogue, Young Israel Congregation, one mile away. It is a hot, humid, St. Louis day, and we are not used to this weather. Nine-year-old Steven, sweating profusely, decides to go on strike half way there. He stops, sits down on the sidewalk, and says, "I am not going on. I am not taking another step. I am staying right here." Though we persuade him to change his mind, he is a very grumpy little boy by the time we arrive at the synagogue.

Monday, Memorial Day. We rent a townhouse in University City within easy walking distance of Young Israel. We enroll the children in their new school, the Epstein Hebrew Academy, and drive around the area. We are impressed. In Pittsburgh, we live in the city. Here, we will live in the suburbs for the first time. Everything seems so new and clean. Our townhouse complex even has a swimming pool, which the children cannot wait to try out.

Back in Pittsburgh, we start getting ready to sell our house, pack, and make all the necessary arrangements for our move. In the middle of all these activities, Howard receives a letter of acceptance for a prestigious special program for Jewish educators at New York University. Only a few individuals are chosen from among the many across the United States who apply. It is a big honor. This program will also speed up the writing of his thesis, *Designing a Program for Teaching Jewish Ethics in the Senior High School: Rationale and Proposal,* which is already approved.

The proverbial fly in the ointment? For two summers in a row, Howard will have to spend six weeks in New York City, starting July first of this year. As we plan to move in the middle of June, it means Howard will literally drop us off in St. Louis and leave for New York a week or two later.

That is exactly what happens. We move into our townhouse in University City, and, ten days later, Howard is gone. I am stuck alone with the children in a new city, where I hardly know anyone. Well, I am not about to sit and mope. I enroll the children in the Jewish Community Center (JCC) day camp, which will start the middle of July. In the mean-time, I buy a Missouri travel guide, and every other day the three of us—Sarah, Steven, and I—explore the state. We drive to Daniel Boone's house, to Onondaga Caves, to the Meramec Caverns, and to the bluffs overlooking the Missis-sippi. On alternate days, we unpack boxes, go to the pool, and walk around our new neighborhood.

When school starts in September, I am worried about ten-year-old Sarah. She has already moved six times in her young life. How will she handle another change? Will she be able to make friends? She has a strong personality and tends to be a loner. I am less worried about Steven. He seems to make friends easily and is more of a people person. How wrong I am! It turns out that the opposite happens. Sarah ends up having a much easier time adapting to the new school, classmates, and teachers than Steven does.

Even before our move to St. Louis, I had decided not to look for a job that first year. I need to devote my time to getting settled and to making sure the children are adjusted, since I know that Howard will again be spending every free minute writing his thesis. Once the school year starts, Sarah and Steven are gone during the day, Howard is as busy as I predicted, and I feel lost. I do some research for Howard's thesis; I enroll in a couple of classes at the JCC; but I am empty, restless. I make a few friends—young Jewish resi-dents' wives who live in the complex— but, all in all, it is a very difficult year for me.

I do apply for the Missouri teaching certificate, which I receive for French and German, and sign up as a substitute teacher with the University City School District. I hate that job. Most of the time, I sub in subjects for which I am unqualified. "We just need a certified body in the classroom," I am told. "You do not have to do anything; just keep order." Easier said than done. Eventually, I decide it is not worth getting a call at six in the morning and rushing out to try to keep a group of unruly kids under control. I quit.

Then, I try to teach for the Berlitz Foreign Language School. They require training in their methodology, which is not a big challenge. Teaching is a one-on-one situation with motivated adults who pay handsomely for the course. Since instruction takes place in the late afternoon or evening, however, I need to hire a baby-sitter. I soon discover that my paycheck barely covers that expense. It is just not worthwhile. Besides, the supervisor in Berlitz eavesdrops on the intercom to make sure I follow the program correctly. I do not feel comfortable and quit, again.

For couple of semesters, I teach a class in Holocaust literature in the Jewish Afternoon High School, which Howard has started here in St. Louis. This is a very interesting and rewarding experience. The students are motivated and bright, and I receive a lot of positive feedback. I also teach classes at the Jewish Adult Institute and give occasional workshops on foreign language methodology to teachers of Hebrew.

Spring 1973. I start looking for a permanent, part-time teaching position. I am not ready for a full-time job. I want to have more time for the family. Still relatively new to the area and ignorant of the various school systems, I take a map of St. Louis, draw a circle around the circumference I am willing to drive, find the appropriate school districts, and apply to each one, as well as to the local colleges. The responses are disappointing at best. I either receive a rejection note—"Thank you for applying, but..."—or no response at all.

The head of the German Department at Washington University does want to talk to me. He actually offers me quite a nice deal. I could enroll in a PhD program in German literature with full tuition covered, be his assistant, teach one or two classes per semester, and receive a small salary. At another point in my life, I would have grabbed that offer. I love literature. But, this is the wrong time for such a venture. One PhD candidate in the family is more than enough, and what practical benefit would such a degree offer me? So, reluctantly, I decline.

Then, one evening, at around nine o'clock, I get a phone call. The caller is the foreign-language coordinator for the Parkway School District. "Are you still interested in a job?" Am I ever! I interview with him, and I am sent to Parkway North Junior High, where there is a half-time position teaching German. I interview with the principal, Mr. Neil, and the chairman of the foreign language department, Tom Thompson.

The moment Tom and I meet, we click. We actually play a game during that interview. He asks me specific questions about methodology and ways to interest the students; I know exactly what answers he expects to hear and respond accordingly. He, in turn, also realizes what I am doing. I am hired on the spot for the 1973-74 school year. Years later, Tom and I discuss that interview, laugh about it, and confirm that both our intuitions were correct. We each knew what the other was thinking.

For most of my life, I felt that I lived a double life, having to watch what I said and to whom. From early childhood on, I was trained not to disclose family "secrets." During the war, three lives depended on not revealing my father's whereabouts. In my adolescence, I had no close friends to whom I could confide anything. As the wife of a chaplain and rabbi, I could rarely be myself. Howard's reputation required discretion on both our parts. And, later, I needed to be careful, as Howard had a prominent community position.

I soon found that true friends were a rarity. Now, for the first time in my life, working with my colleagues at Parkway North Junior High, and later at the senior high school, I can finally, be myself. Here, I am an anonymous person: no one knows my background; no one cares who I "really" am or who my husband is. I am accepted, make good friends, and soon build a reputation as a respected teacher. Tom and I develop a very close relationship; we are each other's support systems, professionally and personally. He is a person to whom I can turn for help, advice, and understanding. Whenever I come to him with a problem, no matter what the issue, I always leave with some practical options. We both know that some malicious tongues whisper ugly rumors behind our backs. But, as all three of us—Howard, Tom, and I—know that the relationship is purely platonic; we ignore the rumors. Eventually, people get bored, and the gossip stops.

I never do discuss my background in school or the fact that I am a Holocaust survivor. When asked about my accent, I reply that I was born in Poland, lived in Belgium and Germany, and let it go at that. Most people accept it without further questioning. One of the teachers of German origin, remarks one day, "Wait a minute. You are Jewish, aren't you? Born in Poland before the war?" "That is correct." I answer. "I did not know that any Jews survived World War II in Europe, especially in Poland," he says. He is a friendly man, not threatening or pushy. He just wants to know. His words stun me, however. I am not about to discuss my life with him, so I just answer casually, "That is a very long story. Maybe we'll talk about it some other time." I have no intention of doing that at all; I just want him to go away. I feel safe in this anonymous environment; I am an equal among my colleagues. For one of the few times in my life so far, I feel I belong, I am not an outsider, and I do not want to compromise that safety net.

Fall 1974. Howard gets the promotion he was hoping for. He becomes the director of the Central Agency for Jewish Education and, later, its executive vice-president. There are not many duties I am expected to perform with his new position. I do need to do some entertaining, have occasional new board members at our house for brunch, and, with Howard, show up at every Jewish fund-raising function. That means during certain seasons of the year we have a formal dinner to attend almost every Sunday evening. It also often means that we are to sit at the head table, since Howard is usually asked to "bring greetings on behalf of the Central Agency of Jewish Education."

Even though there are no demands on me, I am still in the limelight, a position I do not relish. Many people also assume that, since I am married to a rabbi and Jewish educator, my knowledge of Judaism, customs, and laws is far greater than it actually is. I feel very self-conscious about my lack of knowledge of Judaica. I often feel out of place in the Orthodox environment, but I also know I don't belong in Jewish secular circles. I don't seem to fit anywhere. It takes me many years, until I am in my sixties, before I am comfortable enough to answer an inquiry with, "You are asking the wrong person. You really need to pose that question to my better half. He is the expert."

1975. We move into our new house, and Howard finally earns his PhD. That summer, our family has an important conference. I have the opportunity for a full-time job at Parkway North Junior High. I have built up the German Language Department from three classes to five, and I am asked to teach one French class. I really want to do that but need the family's cooperation. It works. Everyone takes on an extra job so that "Mommy can work full time and get all the benefits denied her as a part-time employee."

Spring 1976. I believe it is that spring that I have my first real Holocaust-related shock. The Jewish Community Center organizes a *Yom HaShoah*, a Holocaust commemoration event. The four of us decide to go. The lobby of the Center is mobbed; people are crowded around the entrance to the auditorium. As we get closer to the door, I realize that several young women and men are pinning a paper yellow star on everyone who enters. I start having an uncomfortable feeling; and, as we arrive at the door and someone tries to pin that star on me, I freak. I refuse to have it attached to me; I start shaking and sobbing. Howard leads me to a chair, but I cannot stop crying. I do not remember whether we leave right away, but I know we do not stay for the whole ceremony. I am too shook up. I have to get out of there.

The interesting thing is that, personally, I never had to wear a star in Tarnow because I was too young. I do not consciously remember seeing anyone wearing the star. Yet, something deep inside me reacted to that sight with violent emotions.

Summer 1976. We celebrate Steven's bar mitzvah. My parents come from Belgium where they now live. My mother-in-law, her sister Lil, Connie, and her family all come in. It is a wonderful affair—nothing grand, but extremely meaningful. I am very happy. It is a great occasion for me to see our son up there on the podium reading from the *Torah*, from the *Prophets*, and giving a speech. My heart is filled with pride and joy.

Summer 1978. My life, again, changes. This time, I have a very difficult time adjusting. Sarah graduates early from high school and is on her way for a year of study in Israel. Steven has graduated from Epstein Hebrew Academy and is going to Chicago to the Hebrew Theological College in Skokie, Illinois, for high school. On the same day, we drop our daughter at the airport and then drive our son to his school in Illinois. Although I am in full agreement with the paths our children are taking and where they are going, I have difficulty coping with the sudden empty nest. Work helps a little. I would probably go crazy if I did not work, but the adjustment is still very hard for me.

As always, I survive that, too. We visit Sarah in Israel during my winter break. She is happy, studies, and has friends. What else could I want for her? When her year is up, she comes back to the States but not to St. Louis. She stays in New York and goes to Barnard, the school that rejected me years ago. She does very well in school, as usual, and finishes her BA in three years, with a major in linguistics.

Steven is doing fine in Skokie. We see him more often, as he comes home whenever school is out. He becomes very involved in the National Council of Synagogue Youth and is elected national treasurer. In 1981, he graduates from high school, and off he goes to Israel for his year of study.

Spring 1982. Howard is able to fulfill one of his dreams: he receives a three-month sabbatical to study in Israel. The plan is for me to take a leave of absence without pay and go along. This does not work out, however. Mr. Neil, my principal, refuses to give me my leave. He claims that he "cannot have a substitute for the last quarter of the school year," and, if I leave, I will be fired. I have no realistic choice. Howard leaves, but I have to stay home. I am very distressed about that. I feel almost the same way I felt in 1965 when Howard was called off in the middle of the night at Fort Bragg. Now, however, I do not have children to care for, nor am I the innocent, frail, little female I was then. Still, I find it extremely distressing to be left home alone. The only positive outcome is that I lose a lot of weight because I am unable to eat. In school, the students are all abuzz. Howard has made arrangements with one of my colleagues who has a flower shop, to bring me a dozen roses every Friday. It is a beautiful surprise for me, but the rumor among the students is that my colleague and I must have a romance going on because he brings me beautiful flowers every Friday. We all enjoy a good laugh when we hear about those rumors.

I take a couple of days off to attend Sarah's college graduation, after which she, too, goes off to Israel to join her father and brother for the summer. I am to follow as soon as possible. Howard and our children are in Israel in June of 1982 when the Lebanon War breaks out. I am alone in the States, while the rest of my family is in a war zone. I call Howard and ask, "Are you coming home?"

"Why? What's wrong?" he asks. It seems that in Jerusalem life goes on as usual. There is no panic, no fear; people live their lives as if nothing were happening—except, of course, that the reservists have been called up and that every man, woman, and young adult is glued to the news on the hour. "How about Sarah and Steven?" I ask. "They are fine. No problem." Howard insists. "Should I still plan to come when school is over?" "Why not?" He asks. "I am telling you; life goes on here in Jerusalem. We do not feel that there is a war going on in the North." So, a couple of weeks later, I am on my way to join my family in Israel.

We spend several beautiful weeks in Jerusalem, even though Howard is always in class, and the children are also busy with studies and friends. Steven is flourishing. He is maturing, taking his studies very seriously; and Sarah enjoys a few weeks of rest and travel.

On the way back to the States, I stop to see my parents in Antwerp, Belgium. I make it my business to see them once a year. They are not doing well. They never did get along, and things have not improved. It is sad that they cannot find common ground after all these years, but there is little I can do. My mother constantly calls me in the States and cries, asking for help. I keep telling her that the only thing I can do is move her to St. Louis, a move she is not willing to make. It is a no-win situation. I do what I can to give her moral support, but aside from that, my options are limited.

Fall 1983. Sarah starts a Master's Degree program in speech pathology at Columbia University in New York. She rents an apartment with a friend. When we visit her, we are shocked. The place is full of cockroaches. They crawl everywhere, on the walls, the ceiling, the floors. I am afraid to go to sleep for fear that they will crawl all over me. Sarah is blasé about this. "This is New York, Mom," she tells me, "You cannot get away from roaches here; you just have to get used to them." Well, she is an adult now and has to make her own decisions. If she is willing to accept roaches as her apartment mates, there is not much we can do about it.

1984. Sarah receives her Master's Degree and tries to get a job. She has a very difficult time. She wants to stay in New York, where there is a large Jewish community, but jobs in her field are scarce if you do not speak Spanish. Her knowledge of German, French, Hebrew, and Arabic is of no help in the Big Apple. So, she decides to try her luck in Israel. Being the enterprising young woman she is, she arranges to stay temporarily with a friend in Jerusalem, packs her bags, and is off. She manages very well. She is hired by Bikur Holim Hospital, rents an apartment, and is quite happy for the next three years

In the meantime, Steven's one year of study in Israel turns into three. He is also doing very well, almost too well. He is influenced by a young rabbi at the school, and in his third year decides he will stay at the school to teach and study. "I do not need a college degree," he tries to assure us. "You can be a very good teacher without any degree, and, if I stay here, they do not require any degrees. This is informal education."

Howard and I respond in unison. "That is out of the question. You will come back to the States and get a college degree. Find a yeshiva, a rabbinical school, which permits you to attend secular studies, as well. That is the only compromise we are willing to make." Luckily, he complies and is accepted at Ner Israel Rabbinical College in Baltimore, Maryland, in a bachelor of Talmudic Law program. Three times a week he attends classes in accounting at local colleges. Howard and I breathe a sigh of relief.

Fall 1984. Steven is studying in Baltimore, but no sooner has he become settled, when we receive another call from our son. "Mom, Dad, sit down. I have important news," he says. "I have decided that it is time for me to get married. Rabbinical students my age are all getting married, and I am

ready to look for a wife." I can hardly catch my breath. My
21-year-old son, who has no practical way to support himself, wants to get married?

A few months later, in June of the following year, he has
found her—the perfect girl. He is in love. He is ready, but
am I? He wants to bring Joy to St. Louis so that we can meet
her. Of course, we agree. What choice do we have? I am very
worried. Who is this girl? How is all this going to work out?
What if we do not get along? What if she does not fit in our
family? I am a nervous wreck as I wait for them to arrive for
the weekend.

It does not take long, however, for both of us to become very fond of Joy. She is a lovely young woman, and we
"adopt" her almost immediately. Steven proposes to her on
Shabbat, and we make their engagement public that evening.
We call Joy's parents, who seem to be a very nice couple, well
known and respected in the Baltimore Jewish community.
Inevitably, a very important topic comes up.

"Mom, Dad, are you willing to help us out financially
until we both finish school? Joy will be getting her bachelor
of science in business in a year, and I am in the process of
studying to become a certified public accountant. Joy's parents will pitch in fifty percent." How can we refuse? They are
so obviously in love, so devoted to each other. She is everything we could wish for a daughter-in-law to be.

In July, we drive to Baltimore for an engagement party,
and on November 5, 1985, we return for the wedding. Sarah
comes in from Israel; my parents from Belgium; my mother-
in-law, Connie, and her family from New York; my brother
Leon's wife from St. Louis. Although we miss Leon, who is

unable ro be there, it is a very happy and emotional day.

The wedding ceremony and reception are conducted in a very traditional Jewish manner. First, the engagement document is signed. The mothers of the bride and groom then break a plate, symbolizing the irreversibility of the engagement. Steven is then led by a group of his friends, who are singing and clapping, to the room where Joy and all the women are waiting. He covers her face with the veil and is escorted back. This is an ancient tradition going back to biblical times: Our forefather, Jacob, was tricked into marrying Leah, the older sister of his beloved Rachel, for whom he had been laboring for seven years. Since then, every Jewish groom covers his bride's face before the ceremony after he determines she is the girl of his dreams.

The ceremony begins. The cantor chants the traditional blessings. Steven pronounces the time-honored formula, "Behold, you are consecrated to me with this ring, according to the laws of Moses and Israel." He places a ring on Joy's index finger; the marriage contract is read in Aramaic and English; the seven special blessings are recited; the glass is broken as a reminder that, even on the happiest occasions, we need to remember the destruction of our Temple in Jerusalem; and our son is a married man.

As I see Steven standing under the *huppah,* the bridal canopy, I cannot help but think how the grandfather I never knew would be proud and happy. After all the horrors we Polish Jews have experienced, here is his great-grandson continuing our Orthodox traditions just the way he would have wanted. The chain has not been broken. Our traditions are being passed on to the next generation.

As soon as the glass is shattered, Steven's friends surround the young couple. Singing and clapping, they escort them into a secluded room. The wedding day is considered a Day of Atonement for the couple. They fast to be cleansed of their sins as individuals before becoming one as a couple. Now, in that room, they have a chance to eat and enjoy a few minutes of privacy before they rejoin the guests. When the newlyweds enter the reception hall, the dancing starts, men with the groom on one side of the room, women with the bride on the other side. This goes on for quite a while. Finally, everyone gets to relax and eat.

Almost thirteen months later, we become the grandparents of a beautiful baby girl. Goldie is born on Saturday, November 22, 1986. We fly to Baltimore as soon as school is out. What a thrill to hold my first grandchild in my arms. I do not think I can describe the feeling. My body and soul are filled with happiness, gratitude, and pride. She is the beginning of a new generation, another link in the chain to which I am privileged to contribute.

Chapter 15: 1986 to 1993
St. Louis, Missouri

Fall **1986.** I receive a frantic call from my mother. "You father is ill. He is in the hospital, in a coma. I do not know what he has. One of you—you or Leon—has to come." Leon, my brother, flies to Antwerp. As a physician, he is better equipped to assess the situation. He comes back a week later. "Our father suffers from bouts of dementia," Leon says. "He will probably need to be in a nursing home, and Mom cannot take care of him. He was in a drug-induced coma because the doctors found it easier to control him. I took him off some of the drugs, but I am not sure what will happen next."

I take a week off for family illness and fly to Belgium. Father is doing better. He does recognize me, but he is weak and needs constant care. I discuss the situation with Mother, and we come to the conclusion that there is only one solution: they have to move to St. Louis. When I return home, I set everything in motion for them to receive an immigration visa. Against every doctor's predictions, Father does recover enough to go home, but everyone agrees that this is only temporary. He will have his ups and downs with the downs becoming more frequent and severe.

It is obvious that my parents absolutely have to come to St. Louis. I apply to the Delcrest Senior Living Center for an apartment for them. The facilities there are small—one-bedroom apartments—a big change from the spacious, beautiful place they have in Antwerp. Mother tells me, however, "I don't care. I am willing to live in one room, as long as I am close to you and Leon."

A few months later, their visa is approved, and now comes the difficult part—the move. It soon becomes obvious that, although my brother is extremely helpful as far as medical care, advice, and decisions are concerned, I am the primary caregiver for our parents. I plan the move with Mother via long-distance phone calls. "You really do not need to stay here more than two weeks for the final preparations," she tells me. "I have hired a woman who is helping me go through all the closets and drawers, decide what I want to take along, what to give away, and what to sell. She will also help me hire a mover and make all necessary arrangements. Mrs. Feldman, our landlady, has been kind enough to allow us to terminate our lease. I will need your help with just a few things. Two weeks should be more than enough. Everything is under control."

I make all the flight reservations, and, when school is out for the summer, I fly to Antwerp. As soon as I arrive, I realize that I have greatly underestimated the task. I find drawers and closets full of "stuff"—documents, clothes, shoes, and linens that have not been organized or sorted. The kitchen cabinets are stacked with dishes, pots, pans, and glasses. After all, my parents have lived in this large, three-bedroom apartment for about twenty years. They are downsizing to a small one-bedroom, and there is no way they can take everything with them. I spend the next ten days going though everything—sorting, making decisions about what to leave and what to take, selling what I can, closing bank accounts, and transferring funds to a bank in St. Louis.

Since the movers demand to be paid as soon as their job is completed, I have to make sure I have enough money left for them. "I got a firm estimate," Mother assures me. "I know exactly how much we need. The movers also told me they need one day to pack, and they will move the crates to their warehouse the next morning so that we can still sleep here. I planned for them to pack on Thursday and load on Friday. We can spend *Shabbat* in a hotel before leaving on Sunday." I am skeptical. "Can they pack all this in one day?" I ask. "Sure," she replies. "One of their men was here. I showed him what I had, and he assured me that this is all the time they need." It all sounds under control.

Thursday morning, the mover comes—one man, two crates. I am astounded. "How can you pack all this in two crates, by yourself, in one day?" I ask. "I am sure I can." He replies. "Just show me what you are packing." As I show the man around the rooms, opening drawers and closet doors, he balks. "There is no way I can do this by myself in one day," he exclaims," I have to call the manager."

He makes the phone call, and then we wait and wait. In the meantime, the packer does not make a move to start working. He just sits and waits, but time does not. I am getting more nervous by the minute. Finally, the manager arrives and insists, "When I asked your mother what she was taking, she just showed me one room, not five! This will take more manpower if we are to finish today and load tomorrow. And," he adds, "It will cost you much more." "How much more?" I inquire "I have transferred all the funds out of the country already, and I have only enough to pay you what is on your estimate. I will have to send you a check for the balance from the States."

"I am not sure that this will be acceptable to my boss," he says. "Our policy is that we have to get paid as soon as the job is completed. But I will call my office and see what I can do." After several calls, discussions, and arguments with some head honcho, he receives the go-ahead to pack. We will be permitted to send a check for the balance. I think the manager feels sorry for me and does what he can to help. Mother and I breathe a sigh of relief. Father is in one of his "out of the world" modes. He sits and stares into space, unaware of what is going on around him.

Several more men arrive and start packing; things are looking up. Later that afternoon, however, the manager from the moving company tells me we have another big problem. My parents live on the seventh floor of the apartment building. The crates have to be lowered through the windows. In that part of the world, space is at a premium and houses are built close together. In order to maximize apartment square footage, hallways are very narrow, and the steep spiral staircases are to be used only in emergencies. Everyone always uses the elevator.

To make moving in or out possible, each house has a special hook installed on the roof so that crates can be moved through the windows with the help of ropes and a pulley. However, a new roof has recently been installed on this particular building, but the hook has not been replaced. The only way to move the large cartons is down the elevator or the staircase. The building owner's permission is necessary for either solution.

I call Mrs. Feldman, the landlady of the apartment. "The building's owner will never allow moving those boxes by elevator or stairs; they have to go out through the windows," she insists. "But that is impossible," replies the moving agent. "There is no hook for the pulley."

"Well, they just forgot to put one in. That is not my problem," is her answer.

I call the building manager, who comes up to assess the situation. "I cannot allow these large cartons to be taken down via the stairways or the elevator. I cannot take the chance on the newly painted walls getting scratched or that the movers may damage the elevator's interior," he tells me very calmly. "Okay," I reply. "What do you suggest we do? How should these boxes be moved?"

"That is not my problem," he says. "You figure it out."

I get angry. "What do you expect me to do? You are telling me what I cannot do, but you are not even trying to help with a solution."

"You are a rude and impudent young lady," he replies. "That is not my problem. Goodbye." And he leaves.

I am at the end of my rope "Fine," I tell Mrs. Feldman. "We'll just leave the boxes in the apartment and go. You do whatever you want with the stuff." Mrs. Feldman jumps. "You cannot do that. I have already rented this place. The new tenants want it painted. They want to move in within a week. You have to remove all your property." "How?" I ask. "That is not my problem," she says again. "The only way out," I repeat, "is for me to leave it all here, unless we receive permission to use the elevator or the stairs."

"I am taking you to the police station," she threatens. "They will take care of you." Figuring that this is not a police matter, I walk with Mrs. Feldman to the police station a couple of blocks away. We both explain the situation to the policeman on duty. The officer looks at her and nonchalantly replies, "What do you expect me to do? This is not a police issue."

When we get back to the apartment, the manager of the moving company is on the scene, as well the building owner's representative. I realize then that I have finally found an ally. The movers want to finish the job. They will not be paid otherwise, and they want to find a solution as much as I do. The two men start arguing, shouting at each other. I cannot keep up as they speak Flemish to each other, rather than French. Finally, reason prevails, and permission is granted to move our crates using the stairway, provided that the walls are covered first and inspected for scratches after the move is complete. I do not know how the men manage to carry these large boxes on their backs down the dark, narrow, spiral stairs from the seventh floor without causing a single scratch on those precious walls, but they do.

It is a hot, June evening when we finally land in St. Louis. I push Father in one wheelchair, while an attendant pushes Mother in another. I am home. I did it! I sigh with relief. I have brought my parents to St. Louis. Mission accomplished ... at least, that is what I think.

It takes a few weeks until my parents can move into the Delcrest. In the meantime, Mother lives with us, Father with Leon. We have to furnish the apartment and wait for their belongings to arrive, but, eventually, I get them settled. Leon takes care of their medical needs, so at least I do not have to deal with that aspect. With all this going on, Sarah has been accepted to a PhD program at the University of Chicago and is returning from Israel. She is her usual independent self and needs little help from me.

I am busy trying to keep my parents, especially Mother, happy, which is no small task. She is very unhappy with everything. She does not like the tiny apartment; she finds it most difficult to get to know anyone; the culture gap is just too wide; she cannot adapt to yet another country. It is one move too many for her. As anxious as she was to be near us, reality is tougher than she expected. Although Father speaks less English than she does, he manages to find a group of bridge players and is relatively happy during the times when he is mentally alert. However, from time to time, he drifts into his own world, becomes totally helpless and unresponsive, and then needs around-the-clock help.

Spring 1988. We become grandparents for the second time. Joy gives birth to a beautiful little boy, Moshe. Of course, we fly in for the *bris*, the circumcision ceremony. It is a joyous event, as another young man enters into the fold of his ancestors.

Later that fall, we receive a call from Jonathan, a young man who had visited Sarah in St. Louis the previous summer. We like him, but more important, he and Sarah seem to connect. "This is Jonathan," the caller asks, "Can I please speak to Rabbi Graber?" I listen attentively to Howard's side of the conversation."

Yes," he says, "I do. I think the two of you are well suited for each other." As he hangs up, Howard tells me, "Jonathan just asked me for permission to ask Sarah to marry him. As you heard, I gave it to him." I am thrilled. My daughter is getting married. Our family is growing.

Silently, I give thanks for all the wonderful things that are happening in my life. The wedding is set for March 12, 1989. Both Sarah and Jonathan want it to take place in Chicago, as that is where both are studying and where all their friends are. I agree, but I am worried. This means that Sarah will have to take care of all the arrangements. In her typical manner, she assures me that she can do it, and she does.

The wedding is beautiful. Sarah has handled all the details with hardly any help from me. My parents are both here, but Father is in a wheelchair and does not seem to realize what is happening around him. Howard's sister, Connie, comes with her husband, Mel. My mother-in-law, who has never flown in her life, decides that the train ride would be too much for her. Sarah tries to persuade her, to no avail.

During the next couple of years, life has many ups and downs for us. A few weeks after the wedding, we receive a call from Mel. Connie has a malignant brain tumor. Despite heroic efforts, surgeries, and experimental medications, Connie passes away on April 25, 1990. Howard is with her and her family when she dies, and I fly in for the funeral. She was 57 years old.

May 21, 1988. Steven and Joy's third child, Chananya, is born. In June, Father who has been getting worse, spends a week in the hospital before being taken to Colony Nursing home in University City.

April 24, 1991. Howard's aunt Lil, his mother's twin sister, literally drops dead of a massive heart attack in her doctor's office. Lil was like a second mother to Howard when he was growing up, and he takes it very hard. We both fly in to New York for another funeral. While we are still in New York, Sarah goes into labor; and, on April 29, Joshua is born. Hardly back from the funeral, we drive to Chicago for the *bris*.

June 28. 1991. Father succumbs. The official cause of death is heart failure; the real cause: his poor body just gave up. The last weeks he was so frail, he could not stand up. Although he always knew us, his mind was in a different world.

Almost all the kids come in for the funeral—Steven and Joy with their three little ones and Sarah with two-month-old Joshua. Jonathan is unable to take off from work. They all stay for the *shiva*—the seven traditional days of mourning. It is comforting to have them here with me. Mother, however, is very despondent. She had become the most devoted and loving wife the year my father was in the nursing home. She sat by his bedside every day from nine to five; nobody could persuade her to take it easy and care for herself.

Now, after the *shiva*, she becomes depressed, loses her will to live, and stops taking her blood pressure medication. In the months that follow, she insists that she has no reason to live. "Nobody needs me," she keeps repeating. "Why live? What reason do I have to get up in the morning? Just to eat another piece of bread?" Even the birth of her fifth great-grandchild, Sarah's beautiful little girl, Esther, born July 9, 1992, cannot lift her spirits. She enjoys the little ones when they come to visit, but her involvement with them is marginal. Even her smile, as she watches the children, has a sad quality to it.

November 12, 1993. We are having our traditional Friday night dinner. Mother is with us, as usual. I pick her up every Friday after school, and she stays with us until Sunday. In the middle of dinner, she tells me that she is not feeling well. She is nauseated. I take her to her room to lie down, but I do not like the way she looks. She is bathed in cold sweat, and her skin feels limp. I call Leon. "Come right over," I tell him. "Mom is not well."

"Call the ambulance," he tells me. "I am on my way to you."

When Leon arrives, the medics are already here. "I think we had better take her to my hospital emergency room. I am not sure what it is, but I don't like it."

Leon calls in one of his friends, a cardiologist, who meets us in the hospital. "Your Mom has had a heart attack. Her arteries are blocked," the doctor tells us. "If we do nothing, she will die. We have two choices: heart bypass or angioplasty."

Leon and I discuss it for a little while. "I do not think that a bypass will work for Mom." Leon says. "She can survive the surgery, but I do not think that she can handle the recovery in her current mindset. I think she should have the angioplasty. There is a slight risk to the procedure, but that risk is minimal. Mom has already had two angioplasties, and she did well," he says. I agree.

As Mother is wheeled to the operating room, she is awake and alert. She has been intubated but tries to talk. She is trying hard to tell me something but finds it difficult. "Not now, Mom," I say, trying to calm her. "You'll tell me later." I kiss her on the forehead as they take her away. That is the last time I see my mother alive. She dies on the operating table. I never will find out what her last words to me would have been.

Chapter 16: 1994
Back in Poland

My need to go to Poland becomes urgent after my mother's death. Ever since I learned about my Jewish background in 1947, I have wanted to make that trip. I was afraid to travel to Poland as long as the Soviets controlled the country, and then life became busy with children and work. Now, I am starting to actively research the possibility of such an undertaking.

During my search, I discover the Hidden Child Foundation, a branch of the Anti-Defamation League in New York. I talk to Ann Shore, its director, and realize that this is exactly the kind of group I need. At first, I am sure that I do not qualify for membership. "I was not really hidden," I tell Ann "I just lived on false papers."

"That is certainly being hidden," she explains. "There are

many ways to be hidden. You definitely belong with us. Furthermore," she continues, "we have an umbrella organization for all who were children during that time: The World Federation of Jewish Child Survivors of the Holocaust. We have annual conferences. You should try to attend if possible."

I can hardly believe my ears. For years, I have been trying to connect with "someone like me." I was not accepted among the "adult" survivors, my parents' generation, and could not find anything in common with second-generation members, children of survivors. Now, speaking with Ann, I connect instantly. I know that I have found my "peers."

A trip to Poland now becomes an obsession. I need to visit the places I have heard about growing up. My parents are gone. I am the last one in our family who experienced the war years. Even if I have few personal memories, I have heard the stories from those who remembered everything all too well. Once I am gone, our family's saga will disappear forever.

As neither Howard nor I are ready to make this trip on our own, I look for a tour that does not travel on *Shabbat* and that provides kosher meals. I also want one that ends in Krakow, in the south of Poland, near Tarnow, so that we can extend our stay and spend some time there. It is no small task to find what I want, but Steven connects me with a rabbi from Baltimore who is putting together a trip that fits my plans exactly.

July 24, 1994. Howard and I join a group of twenty-four men and women for a ten-day trip to Poland. First, we visit places of Jewish interest, small towns and villages where, prior to World War II, fifty to ninety percent of the population was Jewish. In some localities, there remain no traces of any Jewish presence; in others, the only things left of these vibrant communities are cemeteries with a few salvaged tombstones being restored by Jewish philanthropies. In some towns, we find synagogues, dilapidated, boarded-up, or converted into museums or movie houses. In almost every city plaques on buildings explain that these structures used to be *yeshivas*, Jewish religious schools, or a *mikvaots*, Jewish ritual immersion baths.

We visit the death and labor camps: Treblinka, Majdanek, Auschwitz. No picture, film, or documentary could have prepared us for a mountain of human ashes with bones still visible; for a glass casket containing human bones found on the camp premises; for torture chambers only an inhuman mind could have created; for the gas chambers and the crematoria. Nothing could have prepared us for the shock we feel when we read ledgers describing in minute detail how much oil was used for a particular crematorium; what time a transport train full of victims arrived from Vienna, Rome, Warsaw, or Budapest; how heavy the "load" and who the supervisor was. Nothing could have prepared us for the sight of public gallows or the rows of barracks with their wooden bunk "beds," each one shared by five to ten inmates.

In the archives of the Warsaw Jewish Historical Institute, I find a ledger from the Red Cross with my parents' and my names. I discover note cards listing our address, intended for anyone who survived—friend or relative—so that we could reconnect. In Lublin, I come across a building that had housed a Jewish organization that provided food and clothing to survivors after liberation. I remember Father talking about walking there in early 1945 to get some provisions for us.

With the touring part over, our group returns to the States, while Howard and I remain and begin my personal journey. Our first stop is to be Tarnow, of course. However, I have read that there is a small town of Zbititowska Gora, between Krakow and Tarnow. On the outskirts of Zbititowska Gora, in a clearing of the Buszyna Forest, there is supposed to be a memorial dedicated to the memory of murdered Jewish children. Something draws me to that place and insists that we find it.

This is not easy, as no one we meet has any knowledge of any memorial in the vicinity. Finally, one brave soul directs us to the site. We find a large clearing in the forest. As we approach, we find two memorials facing each other—one dedicated to several thousand Jewish children shot here, the other, to several thousand Jewish adults also murdered here, all on June 11, 1942. This was the day after the first deportation from the Tarnow ghetto began, when my three living grandparents were taken away. Since this clearing is only about six miles from my hometown, I realize that I might be standing on the spot where they were shot and buried in a mass grave. After I recover from my emotional turmoil, we say a few psalms and the mourner's prayer, then head for Tarnow.

Tarnow, where Jews have lived since the sixteenth century, is now *Judenrein*—clean of Jews. The only remains of their long history are the cemetery and the stone bimah or altar from the beautiful synagogue, which the Germans burned on November 9, 1939. The stones would not burn, so the bimah stands as a memorial.

Partly because of Father's oral history, partly because Mother had given me the information, I find the apartment where my parents lived and where I was born. An old woman lives here now. She tells me that she moved in at the beginning of 1942, just after my family had been forced to move out. I cannot help wondering whether the massive old furniture in the room once belonged to my parents. I do not dare to ask.

I find the building where my grandfather and father had their store and meet an old watchmaker who remembers "a Jewish watchmaker who had a store there under the big clock," a town landmark. "One day, he just left." I also find the house in the ghetto where my parents and I lived.

In the Jewish cemetery, I search in vain for the grave of my maternal grandmother who died in 1934. I have a picture of the gravestone Mother restored before leaving Poland in 1947. But this cemetery, one of the largest left in Poland, dating from the early 1580s, is overgrown with grass. The neglect and animosity of the post-war residents led to vandalism, destruction, and the theft of many tombstones. Currently, it is being cleared and restored. I leave my grandmother's information with the workers, hoping that they will find the gravestone.

After leaving Tarnow, we take the train to Warsaw. There we find the house in which Mother and I lived for about two years on Aryan papers and where Father was hidden. Even though it is not the actual house because all of Warsaw was bombed in the fall of 1944, it is one rebuilt on the same plot.

Finding the farm in Chyliczki, where we were given refuge after the 1944 revolt, is a larger undertaking. We cannot find the village on any map. Even in nearby Grodzisk Mazowieczkie, the town Father mentions in his oral history, no one has any knowledge of the site. I am almost ready to give up when we find a taxi driver who declares, "Of course I know where Chyliczki is. It is just six kilometers from here."

August 10, 1994. Almost exactly fifty years after Father, Mother, and I arrived at the farm, I am sitting in the now-modernized kitchen. Wladzia, who was sixteen in 1944, still lives here with her husband and son. "Do you remember Pan Andrzej?" I ask when she opens the door and wonders what we want. "Pan Andrzej? Of course, I remember him," comes the answer. "Well, I am little Felusia," I tell her. She cries out in delight, hugs and kisses me, and invites me into her home.

We sit around the table and talk about how "good" the old times had been despite the danger and the shortage of food. "The old people in the village still talk about Pan Andrzej," Wladzia informs me. "He has become a legend here as the man who bathed in the river under the ice in the winter. He had to have a daily bath, not one once a week like we did," she continues. "He would go daily to the nearby river. In the winter, when the river froze, he took a hammer, broke up the ice, washed in the freezing water. He would then run shivering into the house to warm up by the stove; his hair would stand up forming icicles on his head."

"We were one big family," she keeps repeating. "You were our four-year-old little doll, the younger sister to my sister Janina and me. You would crawl to my bed when you were scared, and you would only let Janina comb and braid your beautiful black hair."

According to my parent's accounts, no one in the village, including the Sierocinskis, ever knew that we were Jews. During the war, it was much too dangerous to let anyone even suspect our identities. The German occupiers had very strict rules in Poland regarding the local population. Any Pole caught helping a Jew would be shot with his whole family. On the other hand, any Pole denouncing a Jew to the authorities would be rewarded with extra food rations. Neighbors and villagers all thought us to be Polish refugees from bombed-out Warsaw. Even after liberation, it was dangerous to be a Jew in Poland as there were many incidents of Poles killing Jews even then. So, when Father went back in 1947 to thank the Sieroczinskis and bring them gifts as a token of our appreciation, he did not dare to reveal our Jewish identity.

Before undertaking this trip to Poland, I had promised myself that, should I reconnect with any of the Sieroczinskis, I would tell them that they had saved a Jewish family. It was very important for me that the record be set straight. Along with my trip to Poland, it would provide me with closure to that part of my past.

Now, however, as we sit in this cozy kitchen, Howard asks, "How do you like living under Lech Walensa, the first freely elected president of Poland after the war?" Wladzia's husband angrily yells out, "Lech Walensa is a traitor to the country! He is selling Poland to the Jews." I am startled, I quickly change the subject, and we take leave precipitously. All thoughts of telling them that we are Jews evaporate.

On the train back to Warsaw, I can't help but think of a story my father would often tell when he talked about our time on the farm.

> *"One evening in the winter of 1944/45, some farmers were sitting in the* Sierocinski's *kitchen, living room, dining-room combination. There was very little for the men to do when the fields lay frozen. The conversation drifted to a neighbor's fat Jewish pigs. "Jewish pigs?" I perked up and asked, "How could pigs be Jewish?" One of the old men volunteered to enlighten me, "Last fall, a family—husband, wife, and three children—came to our neighbor, Mr. S., asking for shelter. They claimed to be refugees from Warsaw. Mr. S. just knew they were Jews. He allowed them to spend the night in his barn, then went to the police to denounce them. The SS came, shot the family, and made him bury them. Now, he digs up the bodies, piece by piece and feeds the flesh to his pigs. So, he has not only the fattest pigs in the area, but also the only Jewish pigs."*

Back in the States, it takes me months to recover emotionally from the trip. My brain, my heart, and my soul are full of questions. "Why? Why was the Holocaust allowed to happen? Where was God in all this? Why did He did not intervene, but allowed millions of people to be murdered? What could innocent babies have done to deserve being thrown into a furnace?" And also, "Why was I spared? Why was I saved, while one-and-a-half-million other children were murdered? What do I have to do to deserve the right to be alive, to have children and grandchildren?"

Howard gives me books by various rabbis, historians, and philosophers who have written volumes about those "whys" and about theories on God's presence or lack of it. The bottom line, however, is that there are no answers. The best one is given me by Howard, himself. "We do not know why you were spared," he says. "We will never know. Only God knows. The reason might be that one of your descendants will be a great leader of the Jewish people or do something great for humanity." I cling to this explanation; yet, on *Rosh Hashanah* and *Yom Kippur* that year, I sit in the synagogue unable to open my prayer book, unable to pray. I sit and sob during the long services.

Eventually, I calm down and decide that I must do something. I decide to become involved with the St. Louis Holocaust Museum and Learning Center. As I still work full-time, I cannot make any commitments yet but find that writing helps. I write about my trip to Poland; I write about my feelings. At night, I write in my head; then, in the morning, I sit down at the computer and just type. I pour my heart and soul into the keyboard. It is my therapy. I write for myself. For a very long time, I do not show my writing to anyone.

Chapter 17: 1996 to 2005
St. Louis, Missouri & Poland Again

Spring 1996. The Parkway School District Board decides that it will save a lot of money if "highly-paid" teachers are encouraged to retire. The board offers us a deal, which comes to me like a gift from Heaven. I am burned out. I am ready to retire. As the end of my last year of teaching approaches, I am amazed at the amount of love and respect I receive from my students. Every one of my classes gives me a farewell party. One student makes a wall-hanging quilt for me and has all the kids sign it. I am overwhelmed, and it is with mixed emotions that I say goodbye to "my kids." Yet, I know that I have made the right decision.

I plan to start a business. I want to become a financial organizer, help the elderly or busy, young, two-career families organize their finances, pay their bills, and keep track of their portfolios. Over the next few years, I volunteer with the Jewish Family and Children's Service as a money manager in order to help me decide if I really am up to the task. I am assigned two clients with financial and physical problems. One is elderly, poor, and ill, yet cannot keep from overspending; the other is legally blind. I take care of their bills and their mail, balance their checkbooks, make phone calls, and try to counsel them on how to manage their meager incomes. It is quite rewarding, and I learn a lot while attending workshops co-sponsored by the Lutheran and Jewish Family and Children's Services. I also become the recording secretary, then vice president of my synagogue, and take a tax-preparation course given by H&R Block. As usual, however, "life happens," and my plans to become a businesswoman fall apart.

Summer 1996. My brother, Leon, is diagnosed with kidney cancer. It is a tremendous shock to all of us. On June 17, Leon's fiftieth birthday, we welcome our sixth grandchild, Shlomo. Life has its ups and downs, for sure. The new baby, Steven and Joy's fourth, is named after Father. I am touched by the beautiful speech Steven gives at the *bris* in which he describes my father as the heroic figure he was during the Holocaust.

November 15, 1996. Leon's cancer has spread. He goes to Houston, Texas, for major spine surgery, followed by months of heavy immune therapy. On the day of his operation I start to transcribe Father's oral history.

October 18, 1996. We have our seventh grandchild and third granddaughter, Tovah. She is Sarah and Jonathan's third and is named after my mother. Jonathan gives a beautiful speech recounting my mother's travails during World War II. Another major event in our lives this year is Howard's retirement. We have some issues relating to that for which we need to hire a lawyer.

This also marks a turning point in my life. Up to now, I made sure never to speak for Howard. I never offered an opinion or asked a question when he spoke or was involved in group activities. If I had a question or disagreed with him, I did so privately. I was his support system and, as such, felt obligated to uphold his public image. But before we go to negotiate his retirement terms, I ask him, "Is it okay with you if I speak up during the meeting?" "By all means, yes," he answers. I must do something right during these negotiations because Howard is later asked by his boss, "How is Felicia? Is she satisfied with our agreement?" I never imagined that I could hold my own in a group of lawyers and important executives.

1997. All the events of the past few months have taken a lot of time and energy. My plan to start a business is at first delayed and then finally shelved. I just lose my desire and drive for such an undertaking. Instead, I now become more involved in the Holocaust Center. The current director is not amenable to my efforts. "You are not a real survivor. You do not have your own memories. I cannot allow you to speak in the museum," she tells me. That is not the first time I have heard this, of course. The Spielberg Shoah Foundation had refused to interview me for the same reason, and I hear the same theme repeated by all "adult" survivors I meet. "What do you know? You were just a baby," is the usual retort when I try to start a conversation about the war years. Then, they immediately change the subject or just walk away.

Something in me, however, pushes me to share my story, to talk about Poland and my trip. I ask some friends if they would be interested in hearing my story and invite them to a get-together at our house. Howard arranges for me to speak to his staff and teachers at the Central Agency for Jewish Education. One thing leads to another. I am invited to speak to a synagogue sisterhood in Illinois, to my congregation, to other sisterhoods and men's clubs. When the current museum director leaves, I enroll in the docent training class, and my friend Sarijane and I manage to survive conducting our first tour together in spite of our nervousness.

1999. I start telling my story to school groups at the museum. The new director, Dan Reich, is wonderful. He encourages me, and I am slowly able to go through my talk without having to stop to swallow my tears and compose myself. At the same time, I feel an urgent need to see if there are others in the St. Louis area who were hidden as children during the Holocaust. Sarijane suggests, "Why don't you talk to the *St. Louis Jewish Light,* the local Jewish weekly. Maybe they will be willing to run an article. See what happens." That is exactly what I do.

Linda Mantle, the assistant editor, is very interested in

my story and my search for other "hidden children." She runs a very nice article in the spring while Howard and I are away for Passover. When we return home, there are four messages on my answering machine—all more or less saying the same thing." Wow, I did not know that there were others like me here. I thought I was the only one. Please call me." I call the four women, and we schedule our first meeting in April 1999. There is instant bonding. None of us has met each other before, but it seems that we are five sisters who know each other's thoughts and feelings. One thing we have in common is the same thing I said to Ann Shore, the director of the Hidden Child Foundation, a few years earlier, "I am not sure I really belong in this group because..." Women who join us later echo the feeling. So, we decide to make our motto, "You belong if you feel you belong."

Slowly but surely, our group grows over the next few years. Some who join us were not really children anymore when the war started, some were not hidden; but we never turn anyone away. We accept anyone who wants to join us and feels comfortable. We call our group the Hidden Child/Child Survivor Group of St. Louis and become a chapter of the World Federation of Jewish Child Survivors of the Holocaust. The one thing we are unable to do is to attract male members. Men do not seem to be interested in sharing their feelings or have the need for emotional assistance women do. Over the years, our group will become our "home." We will forge lifelong friendships, support each other, cry, and laugh together. And as we get older and need assistance, we will be there for each other.

Winter 1999. I publish my first "Holocaust-related" article. It is printed in the *Hidden Child Newsletter,* but I refuse to publish it under my full name. The byline reads only "Felicia G." It is titled "Lucky Woman." Of course, some people who come across it recognize me and bring it to the attention of the St. Louis Holocaust Museum, whose assistant director, Brian, wants to print it in the quarterly newsletter. I am shocked. I do not want that, and I make it clear that this is a private matter. Of course, Brian abides by my wishes. I guess I am still in hiding, just as I was four years earlier when I refused to take part in the official dedication of the Learning Center. Even though I had told my story as part of the Center's Oral History Project, I refused to be recognized with the other participants at a reception. I did not even attend.

Back in 1989, Julie Heifetz, who interviewed me for that project, published a book called *Too Young to Remember.* She included my interview but changed all names and locations. I was still invisible unless someone knew me and my story. I agreed to have one of my stories, "Jewish Pigs," read in an annual *Yom Hashoah* commemoration dedicated to child survivors, but declined to read it myself.

Now, ten years later, the Hidden Child/Child Survivor Group I started has done wonders for me. All members rave about how much they profit from our talks, how they have formed friendships and are able to be open, how they talk about events and feelings, without having to explain themselves. I think, however, that I am the one who has profited the most. I came out of my shell; I assume responsibility for the group; and I am no longer reluctant to talk about feelings I have kept hidden for decades. I no longer need to hide behind a pseudonym. In fact, I am almost driven to write, to express myself, my feelings, and emotions.

Later that year, I come across a short blurb in the Hidden Child newsletter asking for stories of child survivors—stories of their lives after liberation. I submit a piece, which is included in an anthology titled *And Life is Changed Forever* published by Wayne State University Press in 2006. The byline, this time, reads Felicia Graber.

Fall 2000. I attend my first Conference of the World Federation of Jewish Child Survivors of the Holocaust in Seattle, Washington. It is a very emotional, cathartic experience. I participate in some workshops in which we are encouraged to express ourselves, to let it all out. We are like a family that has come together after years of separation and is trying to catch up. One workshop in particular has had a powerful effect on me. As we enter the room where this workshop takes place, there is a basket with scarves, hats, stuffed animals, and all kinds of everyday items. When we begin the session, the facilitator asks us to go to the basket one at a time and pick something out.

I balk. "That stuff is not for me," I think. "I'd better leave." But I do not leave. I am mesmerized. I approach the basket when my turn comes and pick out a small stuffed teddy bear. I have no idea why I choose that particular object, and I feel sort of dumb holding this toy. We are then asked to tell why we chose what we did.

I freeze, "What am I going to say? I have no idea why I chose the bear. I have to get out before it is my turn," I think.

But, again, I stay. When my turn comes, I stutter, I do not know why I picked this toy. I never had toys. The only toy I remember is a doll I got after the war, but I never played with her." And, for unknown reasons, I start to sob.

Sometime later, I am in a drugstore with Howard and see a display of Beanie Babies. I want to buy one for myself but am embarrassed. A grown woman, a grandmother, buying a Beanie Baby for herself? That is ridiculous. Yet, I pick up two and go to the register. "How come you are only buying two?" asks Howard, "How about the others? You always buy for all the grandchildren." I take a deep breath and admit, "These are not for the grandchildren; they are for me." Howard looks at me but does not say a word. Since then, he buys me a small stuffed animal from time to time, and I have a whole collection of them perched on my computer monitor.

May 10, 2002. Mother's Day. We are blessed with another beautiful little girl, Aviva, Steven and Joy's fifth. Now, we have four boys and four girls. How lucky can we get? My heart expands with happiness and gratitude for the wonderful family we have. Besides the eight beautiful, healthy grandchildren, both Sarah and Steven have grown to be *Menschen*, true human beings. Sarah is a superb mother, a successful speech therapist. She is the driving force in her family. She works part time, is involved in her children's school and her community; and chauffeurs her brood to ballet, violin lessons, and soccer or tennis practice. Steven has earned a slew of letters after his name in addition to the CPA; he has an

MS and Certified Valuation Analyst (CVA). He has built up a wonderful business all by himself and has been recognized among the top CPAs of Maryland two years in a row.

Spring 2004. We are once again sharing wonderful family events. Joshua celebrates his bar mitzvah along with his twelve-year-old sister, Esther's, bat mitzvah. It is a beautiful family weekend in Cleveland. We had experienced the joy of Goldie's bat mitzvah, as well as Moshe's and Chananya's bar mitzvahs. This one, however, is a double simcha, a joyous, occasion. Joshua is one year older than his sister, and as girls observe their coming of age one year earlier than boys, it is logical to have a dual celebration. Later that summer, we join Sarah and her family in Israel for a second round of bar/bat mitzvah celebrations at the *kotel*, the Western Wall in Jerusalem. We reunite with friends for a beautiful brunch in the garden of an old restaurant. It is also the first time I make a speech, instead of Howard. He is always the speaker for the family, but I take a tip from Sarah, who spoke at the Cleveland festivity, and decide to break the ice. My speech is very well received, and this proves to be another step in my growing and emerging from Howard's shadow.

June 2005. Goldie is finishing her year of study in Israel. I decide that this would be a great time to go to Poland with her. As Sarah and Esther are also interested, the four of us go. This turns into an exciting, draining, at times, tense, physically and emotionally, exhausting trip for four women of three generations visiting seventeen cities.

June 21. We arrive in Warsaw on three different planes, on three different schedules, from three different cities and two different continents. I had spent hours preparing for this trip, collecting information and addresses, organizing kosher meals, and deciding what food we needed to bring with us. I received great help from Sallie, my travel agent, advisor, organizer, and planner.

After that first trip in 1994, I had no intention of ever going back to Poland. I felt that Poland was a Jewish grave-yard and that the so-called rebirth of Polish Jewry was a sad joke. However, as the years passed and my grandchildren grew, I felt the need to expose at least some of them to that part of their heritage. Now, in 2005, I find Poland to be a very different country. She has just been accepted into the European Union and her government, as well as her people, are eager to show everyone that they are truly westernized.

Tourism has become an important industry, especially places related to Polish-Jewish history. We meet Jewish groups from the United States, England, Israel, and South America. Japanese, Koreans, Russians, and Western Europeans come in droves. Municipalities have erected plaques, posters, signs, memorials, and markers to commemorate destroyed Jewish synagogues, cemeteries, and killing places. Concentration camps have become major attractions kept up by the Polish government. Tour guides have to be certified and trained in all facets of Polish-Jewish history and heritage. They are more than eager to help you locate a grave or a house or to facilitate a reunion with rescuers. Some are even instrumental in helping former Polish refugees—Jewish and non-Jewish—to regain their Polish citizenship if they so desire.

Souvenir stands display drawings and paintings of Jewish scenes; wooden statues of Chassidic Jews are available in many sizes and prices. In a large bookstore, reminiscent of Borders or Barnes & Noble, we come across a large display of Polish-language books on Jewish religion, culture, and history. I even find a book by Julian Tuwin, the Polish-Jewish author, my mother's favorite, whose children's poems she used to read to me. The notorious Polish anti-Semitism seems nonexistent or has gone underground. Many Poles are quick to correctly point out that millions of their citizens were also murdered in slave-labor and concentration camps. Some express indirect resentment that most tourists are only interested in Jewish martyrdom and ignore Polish suffering. In the words of one salesgirl, "We also have churches, not only synagogues."

The Jewish community in Poland is growing. Thousands of Jewish babies and toddlers had been taken in and saved by Christian families during the Nazi ocupation. After the war when no one came to reclaim them, they remained with their saviors. Many of those "children" who are now senior citizens are just now discovering their true origins. That discovery comes either due to deathbed confessions by their rescuers, neighbors' gossips, or some chance discovery. Others had hidden their Jewish identity from their children because of the anti-Semitism of the Communist government. Now, they feel safe to "come out of the closet."

Chief Rabbi of Poland, Michael Schudrich, tells truly unbelievable stories of young adults coming to seek guidance and knowledge of the Jewish religion. Many are mysteriously drawn to Judaism and want to convert, just to find out from parents or relatives that they have Jewish roots. So, now in 2005, there are Jewish schools and camps, classes in Jewish culture, even a Jewish monthly, *Midrasz*, the first Jewish periodical since 1968. Jewish museums are everywhere, including the Jewish Historical Museum in Warsaw and the Galizia Museum in Krakow. A new Museum of the History of Polish Jews is to open in the near future, as well as a museum in the former Oscar Schindler Factory. There are also synagogues that have been converted into museums all over the country.

On Saturday morning, we join the services at the Nozyk Synagogue in Warsaw, which is packed with a mixture of *Chassidim*, elderly Holocaust survivors, Orthodox women in *sheitels* (traditional wigs), American United Synagogue Youth, National Council of Synagogue Youth groups, Jewish tourists from all over the world, and curious onlookers. The most surreal is a group of at least a dozen children between the ages of four and six, looking like they came straight out of a photo album about "the lost world of Polish Jewry"— ear locks, knickers, *yarmulkes* for the boys and long-sleeved dresses for the girls—and all speaking Polish. This Shabbat there happens to be a bar mitzvah of the son of the Israeli Consul to Poland. As his family is originally from Yemen, the young man chants the weekly *Torah* portion with traditional Yemenite melodies, which are quite different from the ones we usually hear. All this makes for a unique Shabbat experience.

We visit places of Jewish martyrdom: the camps—Treblinka, Maidanek, Auschwitz; the Warsaw Ghetto memorial; the *Umschlagplatz* from which 800,000 Jews were sent to their deaths; and the Mila 18 memorial, the site of the former headquarters of the Jewish underground that led the Warsaw Ghetto uprising in the spring of 1943. We drive to Wyszkow, the birthplace of Mordechai Anielewitch, the 24-year-old leader of that heroic feat. We stop by Pruszkow, the German Stalag 121 transit camp where my parents and I, along with thousands of Warsaw citizens, were driven by the Germans after the defeat of the Polish Warsaw Uprising in October 1944.

There were supposed to be no Jews left in Warsaw at that time; but my parents and I, as well as many other Jews who were hiding out as Aryans, were caught up in this dragnet. There is a sign on a wall next to the railroad tracks that reads, "Warsaw walked through here in 1944." The four of us continue on to Grodzisk to visit Janina, the only living member of the Sieracziski family, who had given us shelter   .

I had met Janina on my previous trip in 1994. Wladzia had followed us out of the farm after her husband's anti-Semitic outbreak and gone with us to see her sister, Janina. In the eleven years that followed, we corresponded and exchanged gifts, but the issue of my heritage was never broached. In the early 2000s, Wladzia and her husband died, so Janina was now the only remaining member of that family.

Before this second trip, in 2005, I had made a decision that I would not go to see Janina unless she knew we were Jews. I needed to come out of hiding and declare my identity. I decided to do it indirectly. I wrote to her in December 2004 about our trip to Israel and our grandson's bar mitzvah, figuring that she would get the message. I waited three long months, and there was no response from her. I assumed then that our "wonderful, close family relationship" had ended. Accidently, though, I met a Polish Roman Catholic priest who was visiting St. Louis and told him my story. He offered to contact Janina. He wrote her that we were a Jewish family but had to conceal our identity, as it was too dangerous for her family to knowingly shelter us. He also offered her the opportunity to talk with him. Janina called him. I do not know what they talked about, but a couple of weeks later, I received a very warm letter from her. She was so excited that I was coming to Poland, but she gave no indication of what she felt or thought about the fact that I was Jewish.

June 24, 2005. We are here, in Grodzisk. Janina greets us with hugs and kisses; she is so very happy to see us. We sit in her modest two-room apartment; I take both her hands into mine and say, "Janina, I need to tell you that we are Jewish."

"I know that," is her immediate response. "My father took me, my sister, and my mother into the field one day during the war. He told us you were Jews and made us swear by the Holy Mother to keep it a secret. He told us to run and hide if we see German soldiers approaching, because the Germans would kill us all for helping you."

I am stunned. This statement contradicts everything my parents told me over the years, but, at this point, it does not matter anymore. I accept her assertion, and we spend a pleasant afternoon together.

Janina is delighted to meet Sarah, Goldie, and Esther. She still considers me her little sister; and, thus, as she keeps repeating, the girls are her family, too. The five of us go to see the farm where Janina recounts the harsh circumstances under which we all lived during those months. "There were seven of us in the little two-room house. Food was scarce. Whatever was grown and whatever eggs the chicken laid were taken to the market to sell. Each farmer had to turn over a part of his food supply to the German authorities according to a specified quota system. But," she continues, "we all lived as one family. Weather permitting, the men slept in the barn; and we managed to have enough beets, cabbage, and wheat so that we did not starve. We survived, and that is what is important."

The following day, we drive south toward Tarnow, my hometown. On the way, we drive through Zabno, my father's birthplace. We stop in Breszko, where my paternal grandfather was born and both my paternal great-grandparents are buried. Although we find my great-grandmother's name in a book that lists the names of people buried there, we are unable to find her or my great-grandfather's grave.

We pass Dabrowa Tarnowska, birthplace of my maternal grandmother, where we notice a large old synagogue. It is boarded up, condemned, in danger of collapsing. A sign in front proclaims that it will be rebuilt and shows a picture of the magnificent former structure. In Tarnow, there are plaques on almost every street corner, commemorating synagogues and community centers, as well as the ghetto. The only building that was not destroyed in the ghetto area is the old, impressive bathhouse, which once housed the *mikvah* because the German soldiers had used it to bathe. A memorial across the street marks the spot from which the first Tarnow citizens were transported to Auschwitz.

Our visit to the Tarnow Jewish cemetery is an experience in itself. I had the opportunity to find someone to restore my grandmother's grave after my first trip in 1994. Although I have a picture of the restored grave, it still takes us about two hours to find it and another forty-five minutes for Goldie and Esther to clear the weeds so that we can come close to the tombstone.

We are in Krakow during the annual Jewish Culture Festival that runs for nine days every June. Events start at eight or nine a.m. and continue past midnight. They include concerts and workshops by famous Jewish artists and cantors from the United States, England, and Israel. There are classes on Jewish rituals, culture, cooking, literature; lectures on *Chassidism*; Jewish music; tours of Jewish cemeteries and exhibits; even Friday night and Saturday morning services. All events are sold out. We attend the Theodore Bikel and Joshua Nelson concerts at the Temple Synagogue. All men are handed *yarmulkes* upon entering, and there is not a vacant seat in the place. The audience consists mostly of young Poles, and I am not sure if there are any other Jews present besides the four of us and the performers.

Thursday, June 30. We go our separate ways. Goldie returns to Israel for a short time, while Sarah and Esther make a side trip to Frankfurt. This is Sarah's personal journey back to the place of her birth. I return to St. Louis, feeling I accomplished an important task in passing on our family's legacy and hoping that my two granddaughters will pass on some of what they learned to their children.

Chapter 18: 2006,
St. Louis, Missouri

A member of our Child Survivor Group dies after a prolonged fight with cancer. This is the first death in our group and reality hits. We are all getting old. Who is going to carry on our stories? Is the memory of the Holocaust going to die with us? What can we do to prevent this from happening? There is only one answer: our children and grandchildren, the second and third generations, as we call them, have to be encouraged to become the link to future generations.

My friend, Bea, and I set up a meeting and call a few people. I encounter many negative reactions. "This will never work, Felicia. We had a group like that years ago, and it went nowhere. Young people are busy with families, jobs, careers; they have neither the time nor the interest for the past." I am adamant.

"Times are changing," I insist." Those young people who were not interested twenty years ago are getting older, too. I remember how I was not interested when I was young; but, as you get older, you find that you do want to connect with your roots. Besides, we now have the third generation, the grandchildren, who are sometimes much more inclined to listen. They are more removed. They are better able to talk to their grandparents without feeling dread about bringing up unmentionable, hidden memories. We have to give it a try."

That first meeting is quite successful. We find two or three "young people" who are interested. They, in turn, know others, friends and former schoolmates. We put together a list of names, place an ad in the *St. Louis Jewish Light*, and make some phone calls. A few weeks later, about thirty people show up at the meeting to start this new group, which they name St. Louis Descendants of the Holocaust. We hold a couple of successful events. We have a committee that meets once a month to plan, and, very slowly but surely, the group secures a foothold in the St. Louis Jewish community.

June 2006. I get a phone call. "Felicia," says Sandie, the administrator of our synagogue. "Could you do us—Nusach Hari Congregation—a favor?" Cautiously, I answer, "If I can, sure."

"Would you consider accepting being honored as our *Aishes Chayil,* our Woman of Valor, at our annual dinner on Sunday, December third?" I am speechless. "Me? What did I ever do? I think you have the wrong person. I do not deserve this. I cannot even imagine why you are asking me."

"You are so wrong," Sandie responds. "We have been thinking and considering candidates. Then, I heard you speak at our *Yom Hashoah*, the Holocaust Commemoration program in April, and it hit me that you are our perfect candidate. I brought up the idea to our committee, and everyone, without exception, was enthusiastic about you."

I still cannot believe it. It had never entered my mind that I could be the recipient of such an honor. My heart pumps hard, and I cannot think of what to say. "Please consider it," Sandie says, interrupting my racing thoughts. Slowly, somewhat reluctantly, I counter, "Let me think about it and discuss it with Howard. When do you need an answer?"

"As soon as possible," she tells me.

My head is spinning as I hang up the telephone. I do not know what to think, but I know down deep in my heart that my ego will not allow me to refuse. As unexpected and unbelievable as it is, I cannot pass on this one. So, a few days later, I call Sandie and accept, as graciously as I can. And the wheels are set in motion. First, I make calls to Sarah and Steven. "Keep the weekend of December first free," I tell them. "Your mother has just become a Woman of Valor. I want all of you to come—you, your spouses, and, of course, all eight of the grandchildren. Make your plane reservations as soon as possible."

The 2006 High Holy Days come and go, the invitations for the annual dinner arrive, and I start planning for a wonderful family weekend. Everyone is to arrive on Friday, December first. We will celebrate Shabbat together, meaning that I need to set up twelve additional beds and plan Friday night dinner and *Shabbat* lunch for fourteen. And, as has become a tradition when we are all together, we celebrate all of the grandchildren's birthdays, which mean a large birthday cake and small birthday gifts for all eight. I throw myself energetically into the preparations.

By Wednesday, November 30, everything is ready. A large roast is in the freezer, all the goodies have been purchased, fancy paper dishes and plastic stemware will make everybody's life easier. I planned for everything—except for the weather. A big ice and snowstorm hits the area on Thursday night. At four o'clock in the morning, Friday, our electricity goes out. No one knows when it will come back on. The airport is closed. No planes can land or take off.

We call the children. "You cannot come today, so let's try for Saturday night or Sunday morning." Howard quickly makes hotel reservations for us. We cannot stay for *Shabbat* in the freezing house. Saturday evening, after *Shabbat* is over, I try to call the house to see if the answering machine will pick up, meaning that electricity is back on. Nothing. We call the kids again. "As disappointed as we are, you cannot come. We have no electricity; we are staying another night at the hotel; we do not know what will happen tomorrow. We have no place to put you up."

Both Sarah and Steven argue with us. They want to be here for the big event in my life. Telephone calls go back and forth until, finally, Steven tells me, "Mom, leave everything up to me. I'll take care of things. This is no longer your problem. "But...." I try to interject. "As I said," Steven interrupts. "This is no longer your problem. I will take care of everything." And he hangs up. Howard and I give up and try to call the house a few more times but to no avail.

Sunday morning, December third, the day I have been looking forward to for months, is here. We are still in the hotel. At seven a.m. I call home again. Nothing. I try again thirty minutes later; same thing. Finally, at around eight or eight-thirty, our machine answers. We have electricity! I am thrilled and sad. My kids won't be here. Just as I think about it and try to come to terms with my disappointment, my cell phone rings. Sarah is on the phone.

"Where are you?" I ask. "We are here at Uncle Leon's house, in Ladue. We just got in. Steven and his family are on their way." I cannot believe it. They are coming after all. Howard and I check out and go home. About thirty minutes later, the doorbell rings, and my grandchildren stream into the house. My first reaction is to hug, kiss, and pick the little ones up and yell out, "I am so happy your parents did not listen to us. I am so happy you are all here."

That evening turns out to be one of the highlights of my life. Steven gives a beautiful speech, representing the family. We are all seated at one big table—Howard, my children, and grandchildren, Leon, who, thank God is now cancer-free; his wife, his son, Eldad, and Danielle, a future new member of the family. The only one who is unable to be there is Leon's younger son, Daniel. In my acceptance speech, I thank everyone, as well as God, for allowing me to live to see this day. I end with the hope that I will be able to see all my grandchildren under the *huppah*, on their wedding days.

There are so many momentous events and ironic twists in my life that I have a hard time believing them, myself. How many times have I been saved from death, from separation from loved ones, and from harm? How many people appeared to help as if sent by some invisible hand? How did my husband show up in Germany, of all places, to literally carry me off into fifty years of happy life? And how did it happen that my two children, both healthy and successful, have married well and given us eight beautiful grandchildren? It truly feels as if someone is watching over me and gently directing my life.

The ironies? I, the fervent, pious Catholic, married an Orthodox rabbi, raised two Orthodox Jewish children whose lives have become much more traditional than mine. I, who used to be terrified at the sight of any uniform, who had nightmares about marching soldiers, married an army man who wore his army dress blues at our wedding. I, whose burning desire as a teenager was to get away from Germany, was later to use my knowledge of that language as a marketable skill to help support my family.

Through it all, I became stronger; though, even now, as I approach my seventieth birthday, I still struggle with questions about why I was allowed to survive. I also wonder, "Will I ever really grow up? Is there such a thing as an adult?"

I know that there are no answers to these questions, so all I can do is keep reminding myself to be thankful and grateful to God for the good life I have had, for my children and grandchildren, and for the continuing love and companionship that binds me to my husband.

It has truly been an amazing journey.

Postscript

– Le Lac par Alphonse de Lamartine (1790-1869)

Ô temps, suspends ton vol! et vous, heures propices
suspendez votre cours:
laissez-nous savourer les rapides délices
des plus beaux de nos jours!

Assez de malheureux ici-bas vous implorent,
coulez, coulez pour eux;
prenez avec leurs jours les soins qui les dévorent,
oubliez les heureux.

Mais je demande en vain quelques moments encore,
le temps m'échappe et fuit;
je dis à cette nuit: Sois plus lente ; et l'aurore
va dissiper la nuit.

– The Lake by Alphonse de Lamartine (1790-1869)

O time, suspend your flight! and you, blissful hours,
suspend your haste:
let us savor the short-lived delights
of our finest days

There are enough poor souls down here who beg you--
rush, rush for them;
take with their days the suffering that devour them--
forget the happy people.

But I ask in vain for a few more moments,
time escapes me and bolts,
I say to this night: Be slower; and dawn
already comes to melt the night.

Made in the USA
Middletown, DE
21 July 2023

35460202R00104